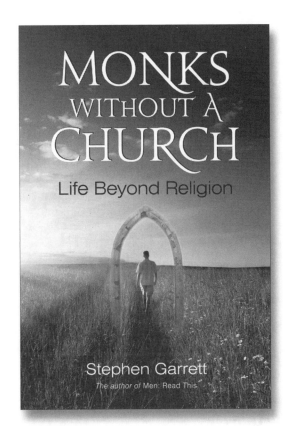

MONKS
WITHOUT A
CHURCH

Life Beyond Religion

Stephen Garrett
The author of Men: Read This

Just Alive Consulting
20435 91A Avenue
Langley, BC V1M 1B4

Dedication

To my Wife Sonora

To my children

To my mother Marge

To my family at large

I love you and thanks for your *everythings*

Stephen
July 2009

– Monks Without a Church –
Life Beyond Religion!

Table of Contents

– Monks Without a Church –
Life Beyond Religion

I was an alter boy and member of my church choir when I was young. I had a picture of Jesus at the head of my bed. I really loved church, prayer, song and people. I thought and felt that church was a good thing and that I would find answers to my questions about life, love and Great Mystery.

All the sermons and Sunday school lessons in my early years were good as my questions were pretty basic and my love of Great Mystery was huge. Around the age of thirteen though, my innocent view of church and religion was altered once and for all.

I saw life and church happening almost separately of each other. People were different in church than they were in their life away from church. I didn't like what I saw and the gap between what was taught at church and what was lived in life was too much for me to tolerate.

I remember once being in church watching everyone head up front to take communion, you know that wine and cracker thing. On the way up many of them looked ashamed or guilty and yet on the way back to their seats they seemed to have been magically transformed looking somewhat holier than thou. It all seemed too weird to me - shallow and a bit of a lie.

I quit church.

Though church served me well and built a good foundation, for me it wasn't enough. I spent the next several decades searching for answers to my basic questions:

Who am I?
Who are all these other people?
What is life really all about?
What the heck is sex, really?
Is there a God?
Where the hell is the Garden of Eden?
Why should I follow the doctrine of any religion?
Where did religion come from anyway?
Is there really heaven and hell?
I started to wonder why some folks like Jesus got all the headline news - What's with that?

These are questions that may or may not be asked in church and may generally be answered in a prescribed or dogmatic way by the priest, minister or rabbi. These religious leaders rely mostly on the 'word' of their religion and have confused the 'word' with the real experience had by folks like Jesus and Buddha. This book is about the answers I discovered in my personal journey to uncover the Truth of Life, Sex, Money, and The Great Mystery. This book explains why I believe that there is an amazingly ecstatic life well beyond the structure of religion.

You see religion has devolved over the decades into a power and control issue! Religions, most of them anyway, do not teach you how to find The Great Mystery yourself because they need to keep you tethered to their written truth for purely business reasons.

Most religions deny the fact that you as an individual human being have an already existing, unique and very intimate relationship with The Great Mystery. Your personal relationship with this Great Mystery is way beyond justifying or defending, it just simply is.

You don't need an introduction to be with It, nor anybody's permission to commune with the Divine. You are already intimately one with The Great Mystery! There are ways to experience Truth directly. Ways that need to be taught in church.

The teachings and techniques I have discovered will set you all free to be your own leader, your own guru and will get you in touch with the experience had by our late great saints. Having direct union with the Truth will help you understand the words written by our spiritual leaders. Instead of following the leader and the words ascribed to him or her you will become a leader by knowing for yourself what spiritual Truth really is.

Many religions deny and more accurately squash the power of the feminine, female, women. So much so that the divine and intimate communion available between men and women, a portal to union with the Great Mystery, has been for the most part minimized, shut down, denied and made shameful. Some of the not too well known teachings of Jesus are surfacing. Lo and behold there exists an entire body of spiritual teachings around sacred sexual practices that lead couples to divine Truth. These 'tantric' teachings can be found in many world religions, they are simply very well hidden.

I ask you to open to these two assumptions of mine, explore and practice them in your own life. You will find it is possible to change the old beliefs you are living by. You will feel freer to live your life as you choose, to live as the full expression of the Divine Love you actually are! You will be able to let go of the deeply seated belief that you must follow a leader and that the leader must be a man. You will be free to be the leader of Love and Truth in your own life, your own family, community, country and world.

You will experience first hand the bliss and joy life can be when you allow yourself to venture beyond the safe boundaries of modern day religion.

There is in fact heavenly, ecstatic life available well before death!

Much Love to you
Stephen

Author's Note
God is a loaded word with many beliefs, opinions, ideas and attitudes attached to it. In order to set out anew I have chosen the words Great Mystery to describe that all pervasive force that lives and breathes all things, that which is all things, that which we all are.

– Section One –
What is Enlightenment Anyway?
The Ingredients

The purpose of this book is to point out different ways you can look at personal spiritual growth - a spiritual path, ways based on the reality of our time. This book encourages you to discover your own truths, morals, and values - relying on your own subjective spiritual experiences - your own personal wisdom that flows directly from your unswerving and personal connection with the Great Mystery.

Each and every one of us is already on a Spiritual Path. It is our own unique way home... our individual walk with Truth. There is no one Path, no one way. There is only the way that each one of us finds in our own unique way. You have always been on your Path. You see it is all spiritual, life is spiritual! There is nothing to search for and no Path to get on... you are already on It, you are It!

It doesn't have to be any specific way, nor does it have to follow any religious doctrine. You don't have to play follow the leader anymore... you have your own unique path to walk. Trust this and you will rediscover your own unique already existing relationship with what I call The Great Mystery!

> *"It is important to understand that God doesn't lead all by one path."*
> *~ Teresa Availa*

Union with the Truth, illumination, awakening, mystical experiences, or direct knowing are the most subjective experiences anyone can have.

It is clear to me that these awakenings are more reliable than written words. They are what written words try to describe. This is why we have spiritual books, scripture and philosophy. Men, mostly, have tried to categorize, systematize, and organize the mystical. This is the source of all religions. Someone had an awakening and wanted others to follow the way home, to share their experience of home. They and their close colleagues wrote it all down, initially to share. And as time passed and the original experience faded into history the 'word' took over as the Truth.

Here is the simple thing. My own personal mystical experiences have helped me understand the depth of knowing that many of our spiritual leaders have been trying to explain for thousands of years. You too can delve into the Truth and experience what Jesus did and then know the essence of these great saints and scriptures. You can become your own font of knowledge.

Such brilliant thinkers as William James (January 11, 1842 – August 26, 1910) have pointed this out and challenged their peers not to let narrow mindsets prevent an honest and *public* appraisal of these oh so subjective spiritual experiences.

When I was conceived I began as Pure Love.

There was nothing wrong with anything. I was simply Love waiting to be fully expressed in each and every moment. No matter how it looked or what was going on nothing could or can alter the fact that all of me and all of life is Love.

Notice these examples:

Put your attention on a new born baby

Notice an amazing sunset or sunrise.

Remember a peak moment in sports where time seemed to stand still.

Recall a deep loving moment with an intimate partner.

A romp in the park with a favorite pet.

Recall a special Christmas time

Notice all of these and you will remember what I mean. All of us are in fact Pure Love. It is one of those Truths that is well beyond question or the need to defend. There will be moments in life that will return us to the unmistakable Truth that Love is all there is. John Lennon was absolutely correct… Love is all there is!

You see It is all just Love.!

I forgot this Truth as most of us do.

All of life, all of it, was birthed from Love even though we seem to take on a life of our own and give the appearance of being life and death it always was just Love. It is one of the Truths most worth remembering. **Everything, yes everything we experience is born of the Great Mystery! We are always of It and It.**

This book, **Monks Without a Church, Life Beyond Religion**, takes a contemporary look at what waking up spiritually could look like and lead to.

When I was eight or nine years old I can remember lying on my back in the park across the street from my suburban Montreal home looking up at the most blue of summer skies. I remember wondering if the sky ever ended and if there was an end would the end ever end. And what is the point of living for 70 odd years? The world has been around for millions of years so it seemed pointless to me that 70 years of human life was all I had. What is this thing people call God? Does He have an office in the universe somewhere?

I couldn't find answers to these questions back then. Mom and Dad couldn't really help. Church gave me a bunch of things to follow but no real answers I could get my teeth into. In the end I gave up my search and instead chose to enjoy sports, girls and pursue the American Dream!

However, all my questions came rushing back in the early 1990's as I faced my own version of a mid-life crisis – my late sister Jody's sudden and unexpected death. I made a personal vow that her death would not be wasted. I stepped back onto my personal spiritual path and began anew my search for Truth and meaning in life - a search for my own enlightenment; my personal and subjective understanding of what makes this whole thing called life work.

I was fortunate to find many great teachers that supported my personal spiritual growth and evolution; teachers that helped me see what was actually going on. Teachers who were willing to point me in the right direction and fiercely, lovingly, keep my nose to the spiritual grind stone. Since May 5th, 1988 the day my dear sister Jody died, I have learned many things about myself, life and other things that are well worth passing along.

I have over the years spent time in Canada, the United States, Africa, Peru, India, Costa Rica, Italy and Mexico where I journeyed and trained with some amazing heart based shamen, visited some breath-taking sacred sites, and took part in many powerful sacred ceremonies. My adventures in these amazing places opened me so fully to Life, Truth and Love that I have no choice but to write this book and share with you...my discoveries of Love and Spirit, my sense of Ah Yes, and my knowingness of the magic of the Great Mystery of it all.

I now know that each instant, each single solitary moment, contains all that the Universe has to offer! Yes, everything you need and will ever need, everything you can possibly desire is all here at all times simply waiting for you to show up and claim it for yourself.

I know now that I can count on the validity of my own mystical experiences to guide my life in a passionate, loving, intimate and powerful way. I know that I am my own leader!

The Big Why

It struck me several years ago that there must be a way to live an awesome spiritual life without getting caught in the news – fear; the media – how to live and what to have; and the quicksand of religious and political doctrines or beliefs – what I should not do.

**There must be a way to live a life full of
passion, abundance, spontaneity, and spirit NOW!**

Yet the more I travel around, the more I notice people in churches, believers if you will; people at work, systems faithful; and people in life just getting by, the more I understand that many people are living an empty life, stable in a way, very predictable and *deathly* safe. I noticed that for many of us there is a lack of spark, juice, passion, and a lack of genuine Love.

Many of us are suppressed, depressed and holding on for dear life, understandably so given the massive training we all received from our everyday lives. Do you know that the average two year old child receives 432 negative comments directed at them everyday? By the time this child reaches the age of 16 they have endured 2,521,000 negative attacks by people around them. Any wonder most of us are a little weird, shutdown, and depressed?

Even more daunting is the fact that as adults we receive 14,000 media hits each and everyday. How we should look, what we should wear, what we should eat and drink, where we should live, what we should drive and how we should speak. Is it any wonder that as adults we are actually adolescent, childlike and confused?

This holding on, this suppression, this holding back, this fitting in has many of us in a death grip of sorts, living a life that lacks magic, mystery, and joy. Yet at the same time we are yearning so deeply to live a life full of passion and genuine happiness. Many of us are living life in the very grey zone George Orwell foretold in his book 1984!

Many are seemingly caught in the trap of trying fruitlessly to fill up from the outside in. Consumption is eating us alive and squashing our capacity to live with freedom and joy! As I look around with more open eyes here are some of the things I continue to see:

Nice guys with no juice, no fire, no guts and no glory.

Women frustrated to death and not knowing why.

Dull partnerships that are negotiated deals not beautiful intimate relationships.

Children well behaved or out of control, angry for unspoken reasons.

Leaders out of touch with reality and not caring widely enough.

Followers everywhere and no one taking a stand.

People blindly passing each other like ships passing in the dark of night.

The Blame Game with little or no personal responsibility.

No humor, no happiness, no fun.

Shallow or no real love at all.

For the most part there seems to be a heavy somberness evident in most people's lives, a sense that we are doing our best to just to get through this life hoping that there will be some sort of heaven to escape into at death.

If only I:
1. Follow the rules well enough;
2. Go to church once a week and learn to follow the minister's preaching;
3. Listen to the boss, do as she says and follow policy and procedure, conform enough to fit in;
4. Be small enough, quiet enough, big enough or loud enough;
5. Just be plain good enough.

If I do I am sure to be rewarded with some kind of mediocre happiness on earth followed upon my death by some sort of freedom and joy in heaven.

But why I can't have it all now?
Why can't I have heaven on earth, with all the unreasonable
happiness there is each and every moment?

As I explored my life and the Great Mystery I have stumbled across some interesting insights, some powerful wins, some profound realizations and some unbelievable direct or mystical experiences that go a long way to answering this very question.

Because of these realizations I am clear that I do not have to follow any particular leader. If I search instead for the Truth myself I know I can learn to live more fully and spiritually, more spontaneously because I am following my own personal inner knowing of Truth stemming from my own unique relationship with the Great Mystery. I become free to live my life with passion and creativity based on my own deepest heart's knowledge.

It is better to search for the same Truth a spiritual leader has found than to blindly follow him by taking his word for It.

Asleep at the switch.…

Somewhere between your birth and adolescence many of you somehow fell asleep in your own life. For me it was as if I fell out of the now moment as I grew in age. As I moved through the social systems, especially the school system, it seemed the more I learned the further away from spontaneity, passion and truth I slipped - much like falling out of love. Many of us spend much more time living in the future or past and little if any time in the present.

Most of us simply forget that we are Love, Truth, the Great Mystery, Divine or what ever you want to call our natural essence. Life happens. We get distracted by the events and emotions of life. We linger in the past and fret about the future – all the while missing the present moment - that very moment that ecstasy lives in, that life occurs in, that we exist in.

Stephen Mehler, the world renowned Egyptologist has an amazing book entitled From Light into Darkness, it is well worth the read! There is a wonderful piece in Chapter 5, *After the Flood*, where Mehler describes the basis of his beliefs around spirituality and religion;

> *'As I have stated in the last chapter, we believe much communication at the height of the Age of Aten was telepathic, mind-to-mind, awareness and the senses so highly developed that telepathy was the norm. Not only was there not a written language but neither a spoken language – sound was sacred and was only utilized in chanting and singing to maintain high levels of consciousness and optimal health, and to cut and shape and lift stone, but as the twilight*

period moved in these abilities began to fail. It was realized symbols would need to be created and utilized to convey complex understanding and preserve knowledge other than the oral tradition.'

He and several of his colleagues believe that somewhere around 6000 BC the human race was highly intuitive and telepathic – mind to mind, highly developed senses and awareness. There was neither a spoken nor written language. As spoken and written language became common and practiced it is Mehler's belief that we fell from a high state of spirituality into a devolved state of religious life.

The more religions grew and relied upon the written word, the more a small collection of religious leaders began to keep secret the practices that would ultimately lead individuals back to direct knowing of the Truth of themselves – the absolute Truth. In many ways religion became a business with its promise of life after death, safe passage to Heaven or an introduction to God.

The reason I bring it to your attention here is it speaks to my feeling that many of us tend to **devolve** from the point of birth onwards. In other words as we grow up and age, many of us tend to fall further and further away from true spirit and get trapped in the work-a-day world of the American Dream.

For some of us though, Truth seems to 'call' in rather unusual ways, oftentimes in the form of some sort of crisis. At this point you can either begin the process of remembering and opening or fall deeper into the past history or future worries – remaining stuck in a sea of mistaken identity. For those of us who can no longer tolerate the pains of life nor ignore the loud call of truth, a new phase of living kicks in… a questioning phase, a time of internally focused curiosity. A period that could be called the warrior phase of life.

Warrior energy is that energy that rips through illusion, untruth and the shells of life we have built to keep ourselves safe. That energy, when unleashed with heart and good intention, can break down all barriers in the way of living a life based on deep Spiritual Truth. It is the same energy we all use to accomplish our goals and dreams despite things that get in the way... challenges, confusion, finances, and a seeming lack of support. Warrior energy is the vital energy of the universe... it is that energy that gives people spunk and guts.

In this particular phase of spiritual growth Mystical Experiences are common. It is these very experiences that most religions tend to make headlines of - Jesus for example got extreme headlines. Similar experiences are often had by many of us and are regularly missed, misunderstood, ignored or rationalized away not only by ourselves, our families and friends but also by 'higher' authorities.

Mystical Experiences
The experiences from which religions were created.
Mystical experiences are a real challenge to describe as many sages, mystics and philosophers have found.

Here are some well known authors/philosophers who agree that the Truth is difficult to put into words. One of the traps of putting words to mystical experiences is we tend to create 'bibles' and then confuse the words with the real mystical experience. The words themselves seem to take on a life and a power of their own.

Eckhart Tolle in his book, A New Earth writes the following paragraph: (page 25):

> *"Words, no matter whether they are vocalized and made into sounds or remain as unspoken thoughts can cast an almost hypnotic spell on you. You easily loose yourself in them, become hypnotized into implicitly believing that when you have attached a word to something, you know what it is. The fact is: You don't know what it is. You have only covered up the mystery with a label. Everything, a bird, a tree, even a simple stone, and certainly a human being is ultimately unknowable. This is because it has unfathomable depth."*

Leonard Cohen is another brilliant philosopher in the form of a poet and song writer. In his book, Stranger Music, he has written a wonderful piece of prose entitled How to Speak Poetry (page 287):

> *" Take the word butterfly. To use this word it is not necessary to make the voice weigh less than an ounce or equip it with small dusty wings. It is not necessary to invent a sunny day or a field of daffodils. It is not necessary to be in love, or to be in love with butterflies. The word butterfly is not a real butterfly. There is the word and there is the butterfly. If you confuse these two items people have the right to laugh at you. Do not make so much of the word. Are you trying to suggest that you love butterflies more perfectly than anyone else, or really understand their nature? The word butterfly is merely data."*

Both these fine men are saying much the same thing each in their own unique style. There is the event, the mystery, the unfathomable, the unwordable. Next came the words, the data and one should not confuse the data with the real thing. Herein lies the challenge of communicating mystical experiences. Words just cannot do it. They form the report of the mystical experience and are not the experience itself.

The words are not to be confused with the real thing!

In the wonderful book Women of Wisdom, Paula Marvelly writes in her prologue:

> "In order for there to be any real sense of I AM, the eternal subject within all of us, free from dogma and prejudice, there has to be an abandonment of all analytical reasoning and objective knowledge. Only through the realm of direct experience and intuitive sensibility can there ever be a taste of true Self."

Paula speaks in her own unique way of the same dilemma - words being offered in the place of the event itself.

I remember studying Lao Tzu, who by the way did not speak English. He lived in the 6th century BC. Scholars grant him the credit for writing Daodejing (Tao Te Ching). Of course not being able to read Chinese I had to find a translation of his work. I chose 4 copies each translated by a different scholar. I read them all. As I compared each translator's version I noticed subtle and remarkable differences.

It left me with the question…
What did Lao Tzu really say?
What did Jesus really say?
What did Moses actually say?
How about Jehovah?

Unless you were there do you really know? And even then how do you translate the spoken word? Does it mean the same thing to the speaker and the listener? To the author and the reader? Philosopher and student?

Volumes and volumes of words have been written and read over the past several thousand years. It seems to me that we have put way too much stock in the power of the word at the expense of losing complete touch with the initial experience that began the whole thing.

Despite all my reservations about the use of words, I happened to stumble across the work of the late William James. He has done a remarkable job in his book Varieties of Religious Experience. Yes in his book he does use words and many of them, and yet he is on to something. So let's look at how he describes a mystical experience. He uses the following four key points to identify and validate them:

> *"Mystical states, strictly so called, are never merely interruptive. Some memory of their content always remains, and a profound sense of their importance.*
>
> *1) Ineffability* – *means simply that a mystical experience defies expression. No adequate report of its content can be given in words. It follows from this that its quality must be directly experienced; it cannot be imparted or transferred to others.*
>
> *2) Noetic Quality* – *Although so similar to states of feeling, mystical experiences seem to those who experience them to be also states of knowledge. They are states of insight into the depths of truth unplumbed by the discursive intellect.*

*3) **Transiency*** - *Mystical states cannot be sustained for long. Except in rare instances, half an hour or at most an hour or two, seems to be the limit beyond which they fade into the light of common day. Often, when faded, their quality can but imperfectly be reproduced in memory; but when they recur it is recognized; and from one recurrence to another it is susceptible of continuous development in what is felt as inner richness and importance.*

*4) **Passivity*** – *Although the oncoming of mystical states may be facilitated by preliminary voluntary operations, as fixing the attention or going through certain bodily performances, or in other ways which manuals of mysticism prescribe; yet when the characteristic sort of consciousness has set in, the mystic feels as if his own will were in the way."*

The reason I am spending so much time on this topic is to make sure we are all as clear as we can be on what a mystical or direct experience is and what it is not. So we can all be clear on the subjective nature of such experiences and not get trapped into believing that only a precious few humans can have them. I will also share with you some experiences that are not mystical or direct knowing – experiences that were realizations, insights or profound aha moments. It is important to know the differences between the experiences through a via or process and those that are direct union that lack any process at all.

Let's take a look at several of my mystical experiences to see if they hold up to this type of scrutiny. Once done I am sure you will be able to review your life and notice experiences that may carry a similar 'feeling' as those we explore here. This is my wish for you, that you can identify your own personal mystical experiences and give them the value they are due -

that you can recognize your experience is of like value as that of any of our great spiritual leaders.

Here is the thing - Once you have spoken about your experiences it will be much easier for you to live from them more fully in your life. Living your truth will free you from the doctrine that binds many of us powerless to others' opinions of how we should live - religions.

I will describe to you several of my own personal experiences, some direct or mystical experiences and others realizations or insights. I will also provide you with accounts from friends and colleagues who have had direct knowing of the truth in order for you to get a sense of the unique variety of these occurrences.

The main purpose of sharing these personal accounts of direct or mystical experiences is to make it clear that ordinary folks have access to powerful spiritual experiences. These experiences are similar to those had by such folks as Buddha, Mother Teresa, Martin Luther King, Teresa Availa, Lao Tzu, and Jehovah. Secondly I want you to understand that these spiritual experiences are not the exclusive or private territory of enlightened or saintly people.

As you read through these spiritual accounts it may also help you discover for yourself that you have in fact had similar experiences. In this way you may feel a sense of relief and camaraderie that can inspire you to continue on your spiritual path or to get going on a deeper exploration of yourself.

For those of you who have not had an experience like these it may be the inspiration you need to find out where you can go to get involved in this type of important and exciting search.

Mystical Experience 1 - The First of Many

I was successful as an investment professional working for a well know firm on Canada's version of Wall Street – *Bay Street*. I had a sports car, a set of Ping golf clubs, a fine looking fiancé, some money in the bank and some great photos of wonderful holidays. Outwardly I looked happy and successful, like I had my life together. I was a man of success - at least so it appeared on the outside.

I was 39 years old and though I looked happy, inside I was miserable. I was an example of the walking dead, simply going through the motions. I was an example of how far-off track the North American Dream has taken many of us.

It was June 1988 when I awoke from this Rip van Winkle-like slumber. My wake up call was my sister's unexpected death. This was the crisis that shook my life's foundation to its very core.

It had been a challenging time for me since my sister Jody had died. I had begun to question most everything I once took as real and dependable. Jody's death did not make any sense to me. If I were the Great Mystery I would have most certainly killed me off and left my saintly sister Johanna Mary (aka Jody) alive to love as kindly and compassionately as she always had. You see I was a bit of a capitalist boor and did little for anyone other than myself. The Great Mystery had made a huge mistake.

The day of her funeral was profound for me. I remember it as if it were yesterday. I was a pallbearer for her. The church was packed to overflowing out onto the front steps of the church. The funeral motorcade was 120 cars long. The cemetery was crowed by hundreds and hundreds of friends and family – a huge outpouring of love for Jody.

As I was lowering her coffin into the ground I made a personal pledge to spend the rest of my life searching for and living from a much deeper Truth. I was not going to let her death be in vain!

Shortly after Jody's death I enrolled in and completed the Sterling Men's Weekend, June 18 and 19 of 1988, in New York City. The weekend was a huge breakthrough for me. I had never done any kind of personal growth work before, especially with a group of over 200 men I didn't know.

The detail of the weekend is not important, nor is the story that led up to my initial awakening. Everyone who has woken up to their True Nature has their own unique story as you will have. What is important is the fact that I experienced firsthand enlightenment - direct knowingness of who I am, what life is and what others are.

For the sake of your understanding I will describe as best I can what happened, how it felt, and what I learned from this my first nibble on the vast meal called Truth.   I tell this story because most of us think Enlightenment, Kensho, Satori, or Samadhi are the sacred domain of priests, rabbis, ministers and popes – individuals who dedicate their lives to the pursuit of the Great Mystery.

We are WRONG.

Direct knowing, illumination is our birthright! It does not require that we be religious or even ready for such an experience! Being a hopeless failure or wonderful success or anywhere in-between, basically being human is all that seems to be required. This and a touch of Grace can and will create these magical moments.

The weekend Justin Sterling and his staff conducted was highly experiential, based on a build up, breakthrough model of personal development. I had applied myself 150% to all the practices we were asked to do. I was leaving nothing to chance. I was going for the big breakthrough. Whatever happened I was determined to have my life change for the better!

As I understand it now all the emotional releasing I did, all the dumping out of my thoughts and processing that went on for me during my Men's Weekend cleared the way for my eventual and initial dip in to the vast ocean of Truth.

As a teenager I had done some reading of authors like Gibran, Castaneda, Rampa, and Millman and had played with mystical thing like séances. For twenty odd years I had forgotten about my early interest in things other-worldly; at least until Monday evening June 20th, 1988. I had returned from my men's weekend in New York and was enjoying a quiet evening at home with my fiancé. I was feeling extremely open and loving - vulnerable in a way. I was feeling unusually calm and happy, not a worry in the world it seemed.

I had left my apartment on Shutter Street in downtown Toronto and was heading for the St. Lawrence market to buy myself an ice cream cone – a triple-decker vanilla one to be exact. I walked home along the many downtown side streets. I felt happy, unreasonably happy just to be alive. It was as if I had no history, no past and no future… simply me enjoying my vanilla ice cream cone as I walked along George Street.

I stepped off the sidewalk to cross Queen Street and it hit me. It was as if the entire world went into frame freeze except me.

Time stood still - more accurately time did not even exist.

Everything seemed frozen in time and space, and yet everything was totally alive and revealed to me.

Nothing began and nothing ended.

Everything was connected to everything else.

Nothing was separate.

Nothing was solid.

Everything was transparent divine energy in motion.

There was no past or future.

Life was all happening in this very moment.

I knew everything there was to know... everything.

All was illusion and all was real in the same moment.

Every breath was a death and a rebirth, over and over and over.

Then, without notice and in a single breath, life was moving again - as if the world's movie projector had once again began running.

My ice cream cone had completely melted and had run down my arm into a puddle of vanilla goop on the sidewalk. Tears were pouring down my cheeks and my hair was sticking straight up. I must have looked totally crazy, and in that moment I thought I was.

I had no frame of reference for what had just happened. My mind tried to frantically put some logic, some reason to the entire episode. When it couldn't my over active mind tried to make my experience wrong, *some kind of acid flash back* was one such thought. Yet as hard as my mind tried to undermine what had just happened, in my heart of hearts, deep in my spirit I knew I had just experienced something profound and life-changing. I knew I had tasted the Truth Itself.

What was I to do?

I had no way of putting sense to the experience that I had just fallen into. I knew something had happened that was more real than the sidewalk I stood on, and yet I had no language to speak of what I had just *learned*. I was deeply, and profoundly heart-opened with no way to describe It.

It was an emergency of sorts, a spiritual emergency. I had no idea what to do with it, no idea where to go for guidance. In a way I was lost in a sea of Truth with no way to put meaning to it given my current life's experience and my current frame of reference.

Imagine trying to explain this to a friend, family member, or colleague...

Well it was as if everything was connected, connected to me. All smells, all sounds, all sights, all things sensory seemed to be totally happening in me or me in them. There was simply no separation between me and light, me and sound, me and fragrance, me and everything else. I couldn't tell if I was hearing the sound in my head or where the noise originated. It was as if the image I saw was both in me and outside of me at the same time. Everything I had held as separate from me was now totally in me, of me, was me. Feelings of isolation, separation, feeling alone did not exist in this new world I was in. It was all connected.

I understood in this timeless moment all the teachings of the great ones, Jesus, Gandhi, Martin Luther King, Mother Teresa, Lao Tzu, Jehovah.....

I knew everything.... I was living in the Tao for this sweet timeless moment.

I was all things, and all time.

I was absolutely everything and nothing all in the same moment.

Can you just see a business colleague of mine, a conservative businessman listening to this...? *"Holy shit Stephen is off his nut."* Can you see him looking for any way out of the conversation?

Yet there I stood at the corner of George and Queen lit up like a Roman candle, bathing fully in the glory of the Truth, enjoying the same union Buddha had, the same moment Christ had – a divine timeless moment of absolute immersion in the Great Mystery of life.

I tried to explain it to my fiancé, and though she did her best to understand, my explanation was lost in a sea of confusion and misunderstanding. I decided then and there to keep it secret until such time as I could fully understand the depth of what had happened. Imagine that - keeping secret my own awakening when it should have been a huge celebration.

It would be many months, and years later that I would begin, only just, to understand the profundity of what I had experienced – and many years and decades later that I would be able to live it more fully in my life.

Now let's apply James' four point test to my first direct experience of knowingness (a mystical experience). As a reminder of the qualities James wrote and lectured on I have recapped them in italics:

> *Ineffability means simply that a mystical experience defies expression.*
> *No adequate report of its content can be given in words.*

Though I was able to put some words to my experience, the mere limitation of vocabulary handicapped my full expression of what had happened. I was unable to communicate the immensity of the experience, its fullness and magical qualities. How could I possibly describe in words the absolute mystery and magic of the entire universe?

Noetic Quality. They are states of insight into the depths of truth unplumbed by the discursive intellect.

What happened to me was way beyond the limits of my mind. I did not think my way into the learnings that I gained during my experience. There is and was no way to intellectualize these sorts of understandings. I simply could not have figured it out!

Transiency - Mystical states cannot be sustained for long. When they recur it is recognized; and from one recurrence to another it is susceptible of continuous development in what is felt as inner richness and importance.

My direct experience didn't last overly long, perhaps 15 or 20 minutes. The expression of it, putting it into words and sentences and paragraphs did take hours, the experience itself however was short lived. Having had other mystical experiences since then I can say that they all seem to share an ongoing type of learning as if each were a different lesson from the same 'teacher'.

Passivity means once the characteristic sort of consciousness has set in, the mystic feels as if his own will were in the way.

At the end of the day it seemed to me that in fact I did get in my own way. Most of my efforts, my seeking, my desiring, all seemed to be more barriers to direct experience than a help. The experience happened, it seemed, by and of itself and did not require any assistance from me. It was as though once I was out of the pressure cooker (the Men's Weekend) I was more available or open to the truth – less willful effort so to speak.

So I would say by these criteria that my experience was a direct experience or in James' words a mystical experience.

An Explanation

"Through my studies, I have come to understand that truth, specifically spiritual truth, can only be defined as that which one knows, without words to be true. It is silent and requires no defense."

The Shamanic Way of the Bee
~ Simon Buxton

Though this was my first such experience it would not be my last. Also know that each realization, each subsequent awakening, and all enlightenments to follow would be their own distinct event. None would be like the other. Though there is a similar ring to all my experiences, each was totally unique.

Many realizations would come to me in dream realms, during meditation, while driving in my car, when walking or working or at Illumination Intensives. It seems there is no rhyme nor reason for any of these most subjective experiences.

You see this awakening thing is totally personal, so definitely not verifiable, so absolutely subjective and yet so totally real. Simon Buxton's quotation above really does eloquently describe what I am so awkwardly expressing to you here.

I didn't know all this information then. I had no idea what had happened to me so here is what I did.

The mistake I made was to credit the workshop leaders with my experience. I thought they had done something magical to me, that they had in some way opened me up to a great Truth. I became a follower of the workshop leader and dedicated many, many hours of effort to supporting their vision. I became a cult member in a way. I was blinded by the light so to speak, looking for the next big moment.

As my path continued to unfold in front of me I would learn much about mystical experiences and the trap of a charismatic leader. I would learn much about the need for careful awareness – and a sober approach to this kind of magical opening. I was in fact in the ongoing process of being taught some important lessons by the Great Mystery.

What tends to Happen…
Back to the *"Reality"* of Life

Tucking my experience under my belt, keeping it secret, I headed off to work the next morning - 50th floor of First Canadian Place, Burns Fry Ltd, Toronto, Canada. I did my best to get down to business yet I felt like I was living somebody else's life. I recognized all the folks, all the office fittings, the computer screens and the multitude of newspapers - the entire scene was totally familiar to me. It felt like home in a way and yet something was oddly out.

It was as if I was the piece of the puzzle that didn't fit. Remember the multiple choice questions, what one of these four doesn't belong - I felt like I was that one – the misfit. I still knew my way around, what to do, and how to get the job done. It simply felt like it wasn't my job, my career or my journey any longer.

I did my best to ignore these feelings, these indicators that something just wasn't right. It felt like something needed to change. Yet I uselessly tried to ignore all my feelings so I wouldn't have to face changing - so I could feel at home in my life once again.

It was the same sort of feeling I experienced each and every day as I walked to and from work. I knew all the streets and alleys to and from my Shutter Street home, all the shops and restaurants along the way. I knew when people usually left their homes for work, when the shop owners put their signs out on the side walk. It was all very familiar to me and seemed like home. In my body, though was the feeling of not belonging any more. I pushed these feelings further under the carpet and just kept plugging along in my daily life hoping all the while that my life would get back to "normal."

I also noticed that many of my relationships felt different. They sure seemed the same to all my family and friends, yet to me something had shifted big time. It felt like something was missing. I couldn't put my finger on it but there seemed to be a lack. A lack of what, was a mystery to me.

My family hadn't changed, Peter was still Peter, Mom was still Mom and so on. My friends were still themselves and the play of our relationships outwardly seemed the same. Again I felt like the odd man out. I was reminded of the old table hockey games with the players that were stuck on pegs and moved up and down the table. For me it felt like I had been placed on a peg in a game that had be going on for some time and I had just discovered I was playing.

I felt awkward in my new awareness. It was as if I was trying to find my way around in a city with no road signs or map. I knew the general layout but man it was tough getting around!

Though I did my best to carry on with my life as I had planned, it was no longer really working for me. I didn't know what to do or who to talk with about all this. So I did what I was trained to do and I stuffed it down and lived my life as I always had.

It worked for a little while longer.

> *"When I walk in the fields, I am oppressed now and then with an innate feeling that everything I see has meaning, if I could but understand it. And this feeling of being surrounded with truths which I cannot grasp amounts to indescribable awe sometimes... Have you not felt that your real soul was imperceptible to your mental vision, except in a few hallowed moments?"*
> *~ Charles Kingsley*

Another knock at the door
One Monday morning several months later my wake-up call got just a little louder.

I had walked the mile or so to work, it was a bright sunny August morning. I was an early riser and usually one of the first guys into work.

I liked having time to get my day started without the rumble of the others and the noisy office equipment. I would drink my coffee and eat my muffin while scrolling through pages on the news service screens, leafing through the morning papers at the same time.

The office would gradually fill up. By 8:30 in the morning it was the roar of business as usual - telephones ringing off the hook, traders and salesmen yelling and gesturing, buy and sell tickets flying all over the place.

On this day though, something else was in the cards for me. Another one of those 'weird' events took place.

Mystical Experience 2

I had just stood up to get the attention of one of the salesmen on the money market desk. I raised my arm to wave and get his attention. In that moment the entire room seemed to freeze. I stood there in silence, everything motionless, and no one moving, not even a flicker on a television screen. Like a movie video put on pause – the frame was frozen – except of course for me.

I stood there in a breathless calm, frightened somewhat yet very aware and grounded.

As I looked around the trading room full of brokers, salesmen, traders, television screens and a multitude of computers, my eyes fell on my father. He was working for the same company, Burns Fry Ltd., on the same floor, the 50th floor of First Canadian Place, and in the same department Fixed Income as I was. As I gazed at him my entire life played before me. I could see all the twists and turns, all the subconscious choices, all the events that took place to get me here. All the events of my life occurred to have me at this exact place, at this exact time, so I could experience what I needed to learn, so I could let go of the past and move forward in my life.

My path to this exact moment was absolutely clear. There were no mistakes, no wrong turns, and no flukes. My entire life to this point was perfect! Time was standing still just for me it seemed, so I could awaken further to my own life and my own purpose.

I realized right there and then that to this point I had been living my father's life!! A life designed to please him and gain his approval. I did this unknowingly as if I were programmed. Most of the choices I had made up to this point in my life I had made subconsciously - and the result was staring me *dead* in the face.

There I stood in front of my Dad *'dying'* for his acceptance and approval. Living his life, not my own. There was no escaping the obvious - I was totally responsible for where I was at.

You should know that my life was a good one. There was nothing 'wrong' with it. I had some money, a good job, a fine woman, some great friends, a wonderful family - all the stuff successful people have.

What came clear to me in this moment was I wasn't living the life I knew I could live. I wasn't doing what was in my heart. I had something else to do – and I knew it. I just didn't know what exactly. It was enough in this moment to get totally clear that what I had been doing for many years needed to come to an end. It was time for a heartfelt change in the direction my life was heading.

Though my second experience was not induced by a workshop or with the aid of a facilitator it did have a similar flavor as the first. As we did with the first experience let's review this second one and see if it holds up under the scrutiny of James' four key points. I will recap them below to refresh your memory:

> *Ineffability means simply that a mystical experience defies expression. No adequate report of its content can be given in words.*

I was able to put the experience and the fullness of it, its profound impact on me easily into words.

> *Noetic Quality. They are states of insight into the depths of truth unplumbed by the discursive intellect.*

I had the fullness of this experience by simply reviewing my life intellectually. The experience provided a depth of understanding my mind was able to figure out.

> *Transiency - Mystical states cannot be sustained for long. When they recur it is recognized; and from one recurrence to another it is susceptible of continuous development in what is felt as inner richness and importance.*

This experience lasted for what seemed like an eternity and yet was only minutes long. Though it was entirely different than my first experience it had a strangely familiar 'ring' to it. It added significantly to my earlier experience.

Passivity means once the characteristic sort of consciousness has set in,
the mystic feels as if his own will were in the way.

It felt that I had stepped aside from my life and was simply looking in on it as a complete outsider, as if I had a unique vantage point to 'see' my own life's path.

By applying James' criteria to this experience it became clear to me that it was not of the mystical or direct type. It was a profound realization though and greatly helped me to move forward in my life.

To make clear to all of you - Yes, there are these amazing mystical and direct experiences of Truth, no doubt. Experiences that are pure union with no via or process involved – simply the Truth and the Truth seeker in magical union. There are also other experiences that individuals can have that are supportive and helpful and not direct union. These experiences are had by some internal process of reasoning or thinking or seeing or figuring out. They fall into the category of realizations, insights or learnings and are very different than direct experiences.

The sum of these two experiences began to push against the momentum of my life. Yet as powerful as they were, the force of my life's history and habits kept me locked in an internal battle. On the surface I was still the same guy living the same life. As restless as my spirit was I remained stuck in my habitual routine.

Opportunity Knocks
Synchronicity as Usual
I had just met a fellow who was interested in the Sterling Men's Weekend. I was the man responsible for enrollment for the Toronto Division of the

Men's Weekend. He and I agreed to meet at the Hog Town Diner in Toronto's St. Lawrence Market. After a snack and a great conversation I signed him up for the men's weekend and he passed along a card of a friend of his who offered a type of unique counseling session. He suggested it might be of help and the people involved were awesome to hang out with.

He went to his men's weekend and I took the card.

For some reason I carried the card with me to and from work and when at home left it sitting in a prominent place. The card was always there staring me in the face, in a strange way compelling me to take action. I resisted for weeks. Finally one day after a particularly sleepless and restless night I made the long put-off call.

When I hung up the telephone I realized I had made a series of mind clearing appointments with a therapist named Judy. The oddest thing I had ever done.

It was not in my mind that asking for help or getting therapy was a good thing. For me it was a sign of failure or weakness. Yet I felt relieved in some way to know that I was going for support.

The sessions were amazing and I was helped immensely.

More importantly though is through Judy I was introduced to an entire body of spiritual work and to people who would influence my life significantly. This body of work is wrapped around the Enlightenment or Illumination Intensive and its creator is the late Charles Berner who died in June of 2007.

An Explanation

You see what is going on in my life already? I reopened to my path, a path of love and truth. Even though I was unaware of what was going on in my life, magic was happening... chance meetings, deep realizations, and awakenings had begun occurring very spontaneously.

The Great Mystery of it all was doing an amazing job of teaching a new and yet innocent student - me. My Path was unfolding right in front of my very eyes though I had yet to see it clearly.

Remember these points...

I am a regular guy working a 9:00 to 5:00 job on Bay Street.
I am not a monk, or a priest, or a rabbi. I don't even meditate or pray regularly.
I haven't been to church in decades, except for funerals and weddings!

The Great Mystery pours it on
More opportunities to grow and evolve

It was through Judy that I met Anjali and Lawrence, two individuals who are still prominent in my life after more than twenty years! They continue to teach me, though now as a colleague rather than a student.

The community Judy was connected with held a dyad (paired sharing) night every week and she invited me to come and take part in the evening. She also wanted me to meet some of the community members who were involved in learning and teaching the work of the late Charles Berner. It was September or October, 1988 as I recall - a Tuesday evening if memory serves.

There were about ten people there, all of whom I had never met. Introductions and greetings done, the dyad portion of the evening began. The process of doing dyads was clarified so that we new people could get the hang of it and dive right into the communication process.

We were each to choose a partner and a focus question to work on. I picked a question like "Tell me who you are", and sat down across from a woman named Anjali - we would be dyad partners for the next 40 minutes. We shared a dyad together and really hit it off. It felt as if we were long lost friends getting to know each other again.

The evening went by quickly, we all said good night and that was that... at least so I thought.

Judy called later that week to let me know that her teacher Lawrence was coming to town for a month's worth of training courses and would I like to attend. I said sure and we made the arrangements for me to attend all of the trainings that were being offered. I hadn't been so excited in many years!

The first event was an evening talk given by Lawrence. I loved it and was very impressed with this fellow Lawrence. He was exactly on time, articulate, clever, deep and spiritual! Whatever he had I wanted. I dove into to all the workshops whole-heartedly.

The work fit me like a glove and I wanted all of it. I contacted both Judy and Anjali and gathered up as much of Charles Berner's work as I could put my hands on – tapes, manuals, essays, discourses – anything and everything I could get. I began to read and study the material and to this day I still have a hunger for it all!

All this study and my relationship with the community led me to enroll in my first Enlightenment Intensive. It was a 3 1/2 day workshop designed by Charles Berner and led by a local Toronto fellow named Rama. I had no real idea what I was getting into except for the fact that it was a meditation retreat designed to help people experience the Truth of life for themselves.

The enlightenment intensive was based on Zen meditation from the East and North American communication techniques from the west. It was touted to be life changing. The intensive was being held in Stoufville, Ontario in late January 1989. I was off to discover for myself the Truth about life!

The following quote of Basho may help to explain the intent of the Enlightenment Intensive:

> *"I do not seek to follow in the footsteps of wise old men. I seek what they sought."*

The day of the Intensive neared and I began to get cold feet, yet I stayed true to my word and continued to make the necessary arrangements for time off work, a ride up to the site and packing. Next thing I knew I was on my way.

The small farm house was surrounded by snow-covered fields, some beautiful spruce trees and a rickety old farm fence - romantic in a strange way. There were 12 participant plus Rama, the Enlightenment Intensive Master, a cook and two other staff people.

Rama gave an opening talk on Friday night. During this time he told us all about the Enlightenment Intensive meditation technique and the general flow of the workshop process. He kept referring to the goal – direct experience or union with the absolute Truth. He let us know that the value of knowing who you are directly, would help significantly with other therapies and personal growth work… that the foundation of knowing who and what you are was of paramount importance.

He set the tone for the three days of the meditation retreat and then sent us off to bed.

The next morning brought an opening talk and the teaching of the meditation technique – and then the dyad or partnered meditation process. Once Rama completed the opening lecture describing in detail the meditation process, everyone picked a partner and sat down in a dyad and began to do the meditation technique as well as they could.

It was new to me so I had no idea of what it would look like or what I was really supposed to be doing. I just jumped in and did my best. Thankfully the staff was there to guide me and the other participants through the learning phase of the first day of the Intensive.

I won't go into a full description here of how the Intensive unfolded and progressed day by day. If you are really interested in the detail of the Intensive pick up a copy of The Enlightenment Intensive, *Dyad*

Communication as a Tool for Self-Realization, by my friend and colleague Lawrence Noyes. He goes into all the detail of this amazing event.

I was fortunate on my first Intensive to have several mystical or direct experiences. In other spiritual cultures you may hear a direct or mystical experience referred to using these words; samadhi, satori, or kensho. I will do my best to describe these experiences as fully as I can so you can get an idea of the realm of the Truth and a sense of the totally subjective realty I experienced.

You should know that approximately 30% of the people who participate fully in the enlightenment intensive for the full 3 days have one of these mystical or direct experiences. These are very rare phenomena in meditation circles where it is considered a blessing to have such a happening even after many, many years of concentrated solo meditation practice.

Mystical Experience 3 and 4

Sometime during walking contemplation on the morning of the second day I was struck by a lightening bolt of truth. I was physically knocked over into a snow drift where I lay dazed, stunned and totally amazed.

> *For a moment, a glorious instant, a timeless twinkle of an eye I knew I was vast beyond belief. It was as if the entire universe existed in me! It made absolutely no sense, but as I reopened to the truth it just kept pouring into me. I am the space between all things. I am that in which all of life happens in. I am without boundaries. I am pure existence, the consciousness that everything happens in.*

I was struck with an extreme headache as my mind and the direct experience clashed. How I had thought of myself, what I believed about me was totally smashed by what I had just 'learned'. So profound was the truth and so in opposition to my beliefs it was like my entire life's foundation was smashed by this one mystical experience.

No matter how much my history and my mind fought against it, the truth of what I was unrelentingly continued to show up in my contemplation. The absolute certainty I had was mind blowing… I was in fact nothing but space, that empty consciousness in which all existence occurred!

> *There was no question about it. I was the space between all things. In the same instant it was as if I was timeless. I was the tick between the seconds, that absolute place of no time at all. I felt I had always existed and always would.*

I tried to understand my vastness, my timelessness. It was as if all things and all time were in me. I wasn't a speck of history at all, I was what history occurred in. I was totally beyond the restrictions of time and space. Everything was me, occurred in me and yet the essence of me was always and absolutely undisturbed by all of life in all time.

My mind was unable to even begin to understand the immensity of what I had experienced. It was so beyond what I had learned in my everyday life.

Later on the final day of the Intensive during the last walking contemplation I was overcome by another splash in the truth. *I felt the utter divinity of me, the absolute sacredness of who I was. The words that came out of my mouth were "I am a child of God.*

No, no I am God."

I could barely catch my breath; I was stunned by the experience.

I had always thought that God had an office, or was something to bow down to, an absolute authority to which I could pray. But God and I were of the same essence!

What?

Reviewing these experiences in hindsight there was a common thread and each experience, to my mind, fell easily and clearly into the category of mystical or direct experiences. In these two experiences the four key qualities were abundantly present.

> *Ineffability means simply that a mystical experience defies expression.*
> *No adequate report of its content can be given in words.*

Though I did find words to describe each experience the words paled in comparison to the fullness of the event. The words I used in no way fully expressed the magnitude or profundity of the occurrences; it simply isn't possible to put words to the truth… it's kind of like trying to put hurricane Katrina in all her vastness in a tiny perfume bottle!

> *Noetic Quality. They are states of insight into the depths of truth*
> *unplumbed by the discursive intellect.*

In each case there was no way my mind and intellect could have reasoned me to that conclusion, the insights were profound and beyond my then current realm of knowledge and understanding.

Transiency -   Mystical states cannot be sustained for long. When they recur it is recognized; and from one recurrence to another it is susceptible of continuous development in what is felt as inner richness and importance.

Each experience lasted for several minutes, perhaps a little longer. Time sort of warps so it was always difficult to say how long each event went on. The euphoria and energy around the mystical experiences did last for some time, especially as I was describing them as fully as I could to my partners, but the euphoria was not the experience; only a mere side affect.

Passivity means once the characteristic sort of consciousness has set in, the mystic feels as if his own will were in the way.

Each time I fell into direct experience it was as if I had somehow gotten out of the way. It was much like I wanted to be somewhere miles and light years away and then all of a sudden being there looking back at where I came from wondering how the hell I got here.

An Explanation

These two direct experiences were the result of my participating in a workshop process, doing a technique designed to willfully create the optimum environment for union to occur. So in these two cases there was a willful intention and a specific goal. However referring back to my first experience on the streets of downtown Toronto, there was no such intention or use of will. Yet the experience had a similar quality, like different chapters of the same book. Willful or intentional aside, direct experiences occur by the good grace of the Great Mystery, and there is nothing that can be done about it aside from being deeply grateful and humble if you are lucky enough to be graced with a taste of the Truth.

There was a nice closing celebration, we all said thanks and good-bye. I left the Intensive and returned home to my 'normal' life. I had been opened wide to the truth and yet was really unclear about what it all meant; wondering to myself what I was to do with my new 'knowledge'. It was right here and now that my spiritual life truly began.

And Life goes on

So back to the grind I went much as I had done right after my Men's Weekend. All the experiences I had were neatly tucked away under the surface of my Bay Street persona, at least so I thought.

I continued attending the Tuesday night dyad events. I poured over all of Berner's work I could take in, both the written material and the audio cassettes. It was fascinating. I felt like I had come home to a body of study I had always known.

So here is the thing. You can see from my research in this section mystical experiences or direct knowing are more common than many of us have been led to believe. I have been involved in more than 60 Illumination Intensives and served thousands of people, many of whom have had these often thought saintly experiences. And yet most of these occurrences go undetected or misunderstood. Many times what is even worse is these experiences get invalidated by the religious powers that be.

This is exactly why most religions are very limiting!

"The concept of Spiritual Union often occupies a very lofty position, relegated only to saints and enlightened beings. For most of us, entering into union is understood as far beyond our reach, and any thought of obtaining it is quickly shrouded in feelings of unworthiness. Teresa, however, did not share this perspective. She believed there to be varying degree of union that we can all experience. If we keep our faces turned toward God, He can take us into the deepest union of love, both known and unknown on this earth. It is we who place the limits on where we can travel, not God."
~Meagon Don

This is exactly what I have experienced leading Illumination intensives. Person after person, Intensive after Intensive I have personally witnessed people struggle with exactly this issue. Many people I meet at introductory workshops look at me in total disbelief when I talk about direct experience or union with Truth. Most of us have been so well conditioned in this limiting way of thinking that we cannot even allow the possibility of knowing the Great Mystery to directly enter into our consciousness.

Know the Truth in three days? Experience absolute union with the Great Mystery, in North America? Doubt abounds! It is one of our major blocks to experiencing our own unique version of Truth. This is why religious organizations are so powerful, and the Catholic Church is one such power house.

Cult. **1.** religious system, sect, etc., esp. ritualistic. **2 a.** devotion to a person or thing (cult of aestheticism). **3.** fashionable

And yet we each have unlimited and ongoing access to the Truth!

If this is the case why then did Jesus get all the headlines? This is the root core of why most religions come up a little short! They simply deny the fact that each one of us is totally ready and capable of being in absolute union with Truth as Jesus was. Religions insist through their very structure that each of us as individuals need their permission to meet God - that we each need to follow their prescribed pathway home.

No one needs a mediator or an introduction to God.

Most religions deny the fact that we are each already in a totally personal and intimate state of union with God. This uniquely personal relationship is the most subject thing in the world and it is well beyond the need to be justified or defended. It is simply so! So what to do?

How do we encourage the creation of millions of bibles in a way that honors each individual and allows for healthy, loving community sharing of the many millions of ways we can find "God". How do we create families, communities, and organizations that can truly honor each one's unique path Home?

– Section Two –
Enlightenment Does Not Change your Life
Conscious Actions Do.

Things to do and to look out for!

The pressure was building - something had to give. I couldn't stand the fact that I hadn't done anything about changing my life. Even though I wasn't sure how or what, I was pissed that I wasn't doing something to change. It was like my entire career's thrust, my entire life's momentum just kept pushing me along the same old path. If I wanted a change in my life it was becoming painfully obvious I had to be the change agent! I needed to do something differently.

Was I willing to let the habit of my life defeat my desire to live a more full and purposeful life?

The longer I held back from making a decision regarding my career and my life's new purpose the tougher life seemed to get, the more I resented what I was doing. It became unbearable. What I 'knew' versus how I lived was so clearly out of whack that it took my closest friends to get involved in helping me sort it all out!

At one of my weekly men's team meetings a buddy finally demanded I do something different. He suggested volunteer work, (something that I personally felt drawn to do), to experiment with what another work environment might feel like. He also mentioned that a men's hospital down the street was looking for volunteer visitors.

Not knowing exactly what to do, and knowing I could no longer carry on the way my life was going, I accepted the support of some good men. I decided to try my hand as a volunteer visitor at the local Men's Hospital. I applied, successfully completed the interview process, and became a Hospital Volunteer Visitor.

My first assignment was with an amazing 50 year old man named Ted Gregory. Ted was afflicted with MS and had the use of one finger on his right hand and some partial movement of his left arm. He could move his head, and basically nothing below it. Though physically incapable of even the most basic of movements he was mentally sharp as a tack!

I was nervous as hell walking along the sanitized corridor towards Ted's room. I had no idea what I would say or do. I had no idea what this Ted fellow would be like. My guts were turning upside down and to be honest, I was close to turning heels and heading home. Something made me stay and weeks later I was glad that I had.

As I walked towards Ted's bed he rolled his head to the right and with a huge smile said "Good morning Stephen". There was something in his smile that said to me - all would be well. In that moment I totally relaxed.

We chatted for two hours and watched some television, world wrestling federation (WWF) if I recall correctly, one of Ted's favorite time-passers. I left feeling happy in my heart after that initial visit. I was excited and very much looking forward to next Saturday's visit.

As our relationship grew I began talking more care of Ted each visit. Sometimes a shave, other times I would feed him. Each time though we would sit and chat and share stories of life together. It was brilliant.

Though I didn't quit my job right then and there, my amazing experiences with Ted gave me the awareness and confidence that in fact I could do something other than investment banking. It was a powerful step in moving forward in my life.

An Explanation

In personal spiritual growth work we can often put too much emphasis on the goal which in this realm is union with truth. Sometimes our efforts are so focused we can miss what is really going on in our lives. We can pass right on by some amazing learning opportunities – opportunities that are more often referred to as insights, realizations or profound moments. These moments in my estimation are often times more magical than direct union!

Action Speaks louder than Words

> *'Are you prepared to give up the life you have planned for yourself in order to live the life that is waiting for you?'*
> *~Joseph Campbell*

As the pressure to leave my career continued to build inside me I knew there was only one way out - quit my job, follow my heart and trust in a force that was clearly much bigger than me.

So one day I quit.

It took me several weeks to actually talk with my boss. I didn't fully realize what a huge decision I was making. I knew in my heart I had to quit yet I had a lot of trouble taking the steps I needed to move on.

I balked more times than I care to mention. Day after day I set my intention to walk into my boss's office and each day went by without me doing it.

It was a Monday morning at 11:45 am. I watched my boss reach for his suit jacket and head to lunch as he had many times before. This time though it seemed as if a supreme force ran through my body compelling me to leap from my chair. I bolted into Mark's office and blurted out...

"Mark I need to quit!"

With the words now out in public I felt a deep sense of relief. I had finally made a move to live my life more from my deeper awareness of who I really was. My heart was happy even though I felt scared to death and very uncertain of my future. Two weeks later I was free from my career that had spanned some 23 years!

Once I had made this personal choice from my own deepest heart my spiritual growth really took off. You see I was beginning to line my life up with the Truths I had come to understand. As I lined up more in Truth, more Truth began to be revealed to me. In a way it seemed as though the Great Mystery was paying attention to me now that I had begun to stir my own pot!

Fact is that the Great Mystery is always present, always available – constantly offering the totality of the universe to each and every one of us each and every moment! All I had to do was to pay attention to It and act from my own heart's wisdom.

As my spiritual path is uniquely mine, so each persons spiritual path is distinctively their own. I have yet to see one individual's path be identical to someone else's. Each person's path is as unique as their appearance, their history, and their belief system. This being said, though, there are some common practices that are worthy of mention. Here are some of the things I did to align my life with my deepest purpose.

Know that this is not a formula for you to follow. There is no one formula. It is my story with some great tidbits of practical spiritual wisdom - some ideas that may help you with your own personal Path. Know that each of my steps might not work for you as our lives are very different. So use what works for you and leave the rest behind. It would be foolish of you to 'copy' me and hope for the same results.

Remember you are your own leader, trust your own heart, your own inner wisdom.

This is an error that most religions make. Many of them tend to focus on their doctrine and have as there aim that all their parishioners live by their 'policies and procedures'. Oftentimes the basic values and principles these rules are based on are forgotten and left hidden behind the words. In this way many religions limit their parishioners to the role of adolescent followers. They do not make room for unique and individual expressions of love or personal spiritual practices.

Megan Don in her book Falling Into the Arms of God has written a great chapter entitled Your Own Pathway. In this chapter she quotes "There are many roads to enter the Heavenly Father's Kingdom" (John 14:2) . She goes on by writing the following two pieces:

"We are all graced with God's Love in whatever way He chooses to express it – we can only make ourselves ready to receive it. And then it is our responsibility to take it and live in accordance with whatever is required, be it as a gardener tending to the flowers or as a teacher tending to the people."

She continues:

"Although we are not always expected to know what path to travel on, it is through our internal being and not through external methods designed for others that we will find our way."

Her words are powerful reminders to us all that we need to honor our own inner path to Truth and not be trapped by the urge to follow in the footsteps of another bright light.

Some of my Personal Insights for You to Explore
Sometimes a Career Change is Necessary

It is not always true, yet for me I found the tension between how I was living and my deepest heartfelt purpose to be way out of alignment. Yes, I could have stayed on as an investment type and done quite well. For me though it would have been a slow and lingering death and I would have only survived among the ranks of the living dead.

In order for me to feel alive and purposeful I needed to do something that would feed my heart not just my bank account nor satisfy the dreams others may have had for me. I felt finished with my career so I left the corporate arena for the world of social services.

Purpose, for me by the way, is of major importance in my life as it is in any man's or woman's life. One of the biggest problems I have seen with the thousands of men I have worked with is many of them lack purpose or a mission. Most men are busy doing things but aren't REALLY up to much - mostly just paying the bills and getting by.

When I was just paying the bills I knew it! I felt it and the longer I stayed stuck in my comfortable rut the more my life became dull and lifeless. My inspiration dimmed, my internal resentment built and my career became a burden instead of a pleasure. Monday mornings became 'Monday mournings' a real drudgery and many of you know what I mean.

Here is a hint about life purpose. A person's purpose may change, evolve and deepen over time. Remember those Ukrainian dolls - the ones that were stacked inside each other? Purpose will evolve much the same as you remove the outer doll and find another doll inside it. As you work through an initial purpose and in a way burn through the karma or need to achieve that goal or target there will occur a time where satisfaction or its opposite dissatisfaction occurs.

When you hit this stage of your purpose it is a great time to reflect, to review and to re-search your next deeper purpose along your path. Regularly spend time looking at what you are doing in your life and compare it to the deepest truths you know. Make sure you are living from your deepest purpose as it will enliven all you do and all you can be and will infect many of those around you.

Taking a spiritual name

All names are spiritual. I want to make this point clear. My mother and father were divine beings. So any name they would give me would in fact be a spiritual name based on my own family's lineage. The name Stephen stands on the shoulders of my Father Lloyd, on his father's shoulders Joseph and so on down the family line.

However, in the adolescent phase of my maturing spiritually I felt the need to be like other spiritual practioners, I needed to fit in. This was a part of asking for a spiritual name. There is wisdom in choosing a lineage for a while and teachers that help you along the way, and for me this was the other part of asking for a spiritual name. I knew I needed some spiritual coaching. Taking a teacher and being named was of great support for me for many years – and here is why.

The name itself gave me something to grow into, a goal if you will. I was named Parabhakti, a Sanskrit name. Bhakti is a type of yoga, the yoga of devotional love and service to others – one who has practiced bhakti yoga and come into full and lasting union with the Great Mystery is referred to as a parabhakti. My name became my personal spiritual purpose. To serve others to their awakening through devotional loving service.

Ultimately as I grew into a more mature spiritual practioner I recognized two things. In a way I had fulfilled my spiritual name because as I see it I was actually living my name. My purpose in life and my actions in life were pretty much aligned. I felt congruent. What I was doing in the world and my deepest heart's passions were in harmony. In other words my spiritual name really worked for my own personal evolution! I grew into my name.

As I grew in my own spiritual practice I remembered that I do in fact have a personal lineage – it is my family! Lloyd my father, Eric my uncle, Joseph my grandfather and so it goes all the way back to 1784 here in

Canada... Each of these men taught me about certain facets of life! Though they weren't enlightened spiritually, they sure had lots of life wisdom that they passed on to me as best they could; mentally, emotionally, physically, and energetically. They also passed remarkable unspoken wisdom along to me through their genetics!

They taught me about the working world, the world of family and about living and paying my way - all amazing teachings. Through their very example, no matter whether I judged it a good example or a bad example, I learned about life through the perspective of the Garrett men.

Being more aware of my own lineage I realized that taking a spiritual name had two sides to it. One side was the personal growth piece I spoke about a few paragraphs ago. The second side of it was an unconscious escape from the reality of my life – the Stephen piece or the practical side of life, money, sex, and power. In a way I left that all behind to learn and grow spiritually. I have realized that my life is not just one or the other, spiritual life or living in the world – it is BOTH.

The notion or idea that we have separate or divided lives, a sex life, a family life, a spiritual life, a working life, a personal life and a social life is absolute non-sense. We have only one indivisible, unique single solitary life! There is no separation in life at all. It is simply one life, no more no less.

Taking my name Stephen back and keeping the name Parabhakti more as an adjective is my acknowledgement that all my life including money, sex, and power is spiritual and that all people in my life are in fact my teachers! Looking more fully at spiritual naming and the gathering of people around the charismatic guru – the one granting the names – I began noticing some common themes;

Charismatic and powerful leader

Unified inner circle of people surrounding the leader

Loss of personal freedom

The creation of a doctrine

So it is wise to be aware of these themes and make a sober choice when it comes to the taking of spiritual names!

Ask the right Questions…
And be sure to get the answers!

As I continued to grow spiritually my curiosity about key portions of my life naturally arose. I really wanted to understand what was going on in my life and why. One of the questions that arose for me was this one:

Sex is What?

I knew a fair amount about sex, so I thought. I mean after all I did have children! I did know about the basics, procreation, animal instincts, sexual preferences and the act of sex. I wanted to know what the foundation of it was. I was struck by the depth of my curiosity… what is sex really?

So I began to seek out the answer to this seemingly obvious question. I poured through books, web sites, newspaper articles and journals. They were all interesting, some more so than others and yet after all my research I was still left wondering what the pure foundation of sex was.

I had just about given up the search when one day I was leafing through a very old British English dictionary. I had looked up all the regular sex words and found nothing new until I looked up the word intercourse. In this dusty old weathered dictionary lay the answer to my question.

There were the expected definitions there too, but one leapt off the page at me as if the answer was being burned into my brain.

"Communion with God."

I was so shocked I slammed the dictionary shut. Timidly I found my way back to the word "intercourse" to check and see if I was hallucinating or not. There it was again...

"Communion with God."

As I opened to the possibility of this being so, my heart opened wide and all time seemed to stop. I experienced the truth of what I had just read in that moment.

> *All beings are divine so any relating act is communion with Me.*
> *Women are divine as are men so the act of sex is divine union.*
> *Sex drive is amongst other thing a deep desire for union with Me.*
> *Through union with each other you will find Me.*

It was as if The Great Mystery was talking to me.

When time resumed tears were pouring down my face, tears of relief and a profound joy.

Immediately another question popped into my mind... where are the women? What has happened to them? If union of masculine and feminine is in its essence intimate communion as David Deida insists in his book, Intimate Communion, then where the hell has the feminine gone and why was she been banished from spiritual life?

I started to look around and did some basic research on women and religion. I stumbled across several amazing authors who have been asking the same question. Paula Marvelly wrote Women of Wisdom, Eckhart Tolle and his newest book A New Earth and Megan Don and her wonderful book Falling into the Arms of God. And Barbara Wlaker's work The Woman's Encyclopedia. Each of these fine author/philosophers had done some profound digging into the missing spiritual link, women.

Here are some of their discoveries.

Paula Marvelly asserts early on in her book Women of Wisdom that prior to the Bronze Age 3500 years before Christ, Mesopotamia and many other cultures were led and guided by intuitive feminine wisdom. However the notion of a hero or a superhuman male role model came into force, and fear and violence moved to the fore in the form of invasions. Consciousness changed too, as survival and the quest for power - personal power, power of religion, and power of nations took over.

It is Paula's contention that Mother Goddess was ultimately displaced by the separative Father God. Harmony, abundance and peace were replaced by discord, degeneration and war. With this decline of the sacred feminine way back in 3500 BC women in community also saw their role in society deteriorate to a position subordinate to men – in many cultures women became mere possession of men.

Echkart Tolle writes about the same sort of neglect of the feminine in his newest book, A New Earth. He looks at the past two thousand years and notices the same sort of annihilation of women at the hands of the "Holy Inquisition" an institution founded by the Roman Catholic Church. This institution's role was to suppress heresy, and they did so in their way by torturing or killing 3 to 5 million women during a three hundred year period. Tolle explains that women's natural love of animals, nature, and medicinal plants was enough to have them branded as witches.

Other cultures and religions in their own unique ways also suppressed women – Judaism, Islam and Buddhism to name but a few. The status of women, states Tolle, was reduced to being bearers of children and property of men. So devastating was the attack that the suppression of feminine ways has become internalized even in most women.

The Women's Encyclopedia written by Barbara Walker speaks of the same diminishment of women. On page 910 she sites Reverend Doctor Joseph Fletcher who wrote the following:

> *"The Christian Church must shoulder much of the blame for the confusion, ignorance and guilt which surrounds sex in Western culture… from its earliest primitive beginnings swayed many Puritanical people both Catholic and Protestant to view sex as inherently evil."*

He goes on to state that the Christian abhorrence of sex began with the fathers of the church, who insisted that the kingdom of God couldn't be established until the human race was allowed to die out through universal celibacy.

And the research continued to pile up.

Megan Don writes of Teresa of Avila in her book, Falling into the Arms of God. Teresa knew intuitively that the mystery of the divine was available to all people. For her contemplation was not restricted to nuns and monks.

Teresa's divine or mystical experiences were so blissful and ecstatic that the monks of her day were unable to understand them. Priests often told her that these experiences of hers did not issue from God at all. It was the devil, they said, and she was ordered to rebuke them. Yet her experiences continued.

You see the priests (men or masculine energy) did not have these prayerful ecstasies of total absorption (surrender) and could not imagine that God would speak to a soul in such a way. Most men awaken into the openness or emptiness or nothingness that is typically associated with the masculine. Read any of David Deida's books and you will discover how very different women and men are in all aspects of life. So it naturally follows that women and men would and do awaken differently.

Women typically awaken in the space of fullness, bliss and ecstasy. They are everything. It is generally a full mind body spirit experience that can be rich with movement and sensory stimulation. Men and women awaken to The Great Mystery very differently. Even though the Great Mystery they each awaken to is the same, their unique process is like night and day.

So over time women were banished from religion, much to the detriment of our spiritual evolution. This lack of feminine perspective and energy continued to fuel the ongoing devolution of most world religions.

Ongoing Variety of Spiritual Practices

As an athlete, an artist or a performer it is abundantly clear that ongoing practice is one of the major keys to success. Malcolm Gladwell speaks to the impact of practice in his book Outliers.

In the world of Love and Inclusion, practice is also very important. We need to practice the art form of love daily. We also need to sharpen our saw, as Stephen Covey asserts, with other like-spirited people. Here are some ways to stay sharp spiritually and to open more fully your deepest heart:

Daily Awareness Practices

There are many CDs, DVDs and books around that offer you daily practices, so I am not going to delve deeply into practices here. It is important to choose a set of daily practices and do them regularly. One hint is to post your daily practices someplace where you will see them daily... by the fridge, the front door of your home or by your bathroom mirror. Look at your list each and every day and choose one or two practices and just do them. Do this for 3 months straight and see what happens.

Men's or Women's groups

Although practicing on your own is good, having a group of great people around you to support your personal growth is even better. Find a group of people with a similar goal in mind... deeper relationship, creating more abundance, offering more in service, and join them. The ongoing support from people other than immediate family is profoundly helpful in your personal evolution. Others have a more objective view of your progress and where you need more practice – they can see you better than you can see yourself. A great support group is also a wonderful place to offer your own gifts to others, to practice the art of loving and giving of yourself voluntarily.

Keeping the genders separate is very important in that same sex feedback is most often the most helpful feedback you can receive. If you are in a relationship this practice also helps significantly to increase the sexual polarity in your relationship! An added bonus.

Illumination Intensives

One of the most common things that hold us back in life is not knowing clearly who we are or what we are up to in life. The Illumination Intensive, a spiritual boot camp if you will, is one workshop that truly helps in finding out who you are. The Intensive process also helps clear out unnecessary thoughts or stored up emotions so that you can have a less obstructed view of you and your life.

Life also tends to fill you up with unnecessary baggage, incomplete communications with others, emotional withholds and unspoken words. The Illumination Intensive process is a personal house cleaning project that when undertaken once or twice yearly will keep you clear and clean and much more centered and powerful in who you are.

Regular and diverse personal growth workshops

Taking a variety of personal growth workshops is also darn important. Keeping your saw sharp by learning new tools and practices that will help you in your life are some of the best investments you can make for both yourself and everyone around you.

I used to work in the investment business and I found that the last place a person would invest was in themselves! Buy a stock or an investment or a house or a car, some kind of asset no problem, but waste money on me…naw. You are the first place you should invest in!

Sit down now and take a look at your budget and allocate a certain portion of your disposable income to YOU! Then look around and find workshops that have helped people around you grow and develop. Notice people who you admire and ask what they are doing in their life to get ahead, in passion, freedom and abundance creation. Every three or six months make sure you have enrolled in a personal growth workshop that you know will improve your skills and abilities to create more love, freedom and abundance in your life.

Sweat Lodges or Shamanic Ceremonies

Another way to grow and evolve is to get involved in sacred practices of other cultures. Our own first nations' culture is rich with spiritual practice. The sweat lodge is only one such practice. Check out local personal growth magazines and find one or two of the many ceremonies that draw you. Check out the shaman or leader and do so by talking with people who have done work with the shaman. Do your research well and choose a ceremony leader who is what he or she states they are. Trust your intuition on this one. You need to feel that the shaman is totally trustworthy before you get involved. Different doorways open in different ceremonies so widen your choice of possibilities and access to the Great Mystery.

World travels to different cultures and spiritual ways.
If you have the financial means, travel! Find a way to hook up with a group that travels to world sites and fully explores the culture and spirit of the country, not a tourist trip but a spiritual adventure tour if you will. Take a look into the depth of the spiritual culture of the country you are traveling in.

Find a spiritual tour company like WarriorSage that will introduce you to local teachers and shamen of depth and heart - guides who will take you into the spirit of the land and teach you the ceremonies and practice unique to their culture. Broaden your personal understanding of what spiritual means by fully exploring other cultures aside from your own!

Enter the shamen and spirit medicine
Diego, Jorge, Miguel, Hakim, and Hank are but a few of the amazing shamanic teachers I have met on my journeys with WarriorSage. These amazing men have expanded my understanding of life here on the planet and they have supported my personal spiritual growth and knowledge of the Great Mysteries of life and love. I feel as if I have been living in the books of Carlos Castenadas, being toured through the universe by wise and knowing teachers.

The teachings I have received and the learnings I am grateful for are too numerous to mention here. Importantly though they have all aligned with the many mystical experiences I have had. The shamanic realms have fully supported my spiritual growth by filling out in a grand way the direct experiences I had under my own power.

The shamanic realms are wonderful, instructive and glorious. I have learned lots and have been able to integrate some of what I have learned… and this is an important point. Delving into shamanic realms can be intoxicating - the journeys are oftentimes magical and exciting. These shamanic adventures do not always need to include teacher or spirit medicine, often the guidance of a wise shaman is enough to open the portals and part the veils to other worlds. Be cautious, though, as there is always the lure of even more intoxication. Be sober in your use of these realms as they are not a playground, but a spiritual incubator.

Personally I have much to integrate into my life from the past journeys I have traveled and until I am more fully living my realizations I will minimize my use of these gateway openers.

I am indeed blessed.

The Appropriate Use of Spirit Teacher Medicines

Here is another adventure that will help you see that mystical experiences can be and are in fact a natural part of our sacred life. Most of us however are so caught up in surviving life, getting from paycheck to paycheck that we don't even know that we are missing these glorious learning opportunities. We fail to see these unique events or happenings that are in fact occurring regularly everywhere around us.

We simply have our attention on surviving the challenges of life and merely getting by rather than experiencing the magical happenings and unreasonable happiness.

It is important for you to know that Spirit medicine is not drug use or a way to sidestep life and spiritual growth. It is a way that individuals can expand their knowingness of the Great Mystery. In most cultures around the world Spirit Medicine has been used in sacred ceremonies for centuries. Peru, Africa, Mexico, and Ireland, just to name a few are cultures rich in sacred ceremonies. Often these ceremonies went underground to avoid the onslaught of a conqueror's religious cleansing. There has been a rising awareness of these Spirit Medicines and their shamen over the past decade or so and a new light is being shone on the appropriate and sacred use of these wise teacher plants in ceremonies around the world.

It is important to know who you will be working with. Choosing the right shaman or spirit medicine teacher is of the utmost importance as is choosing the right group of people to experience the amazing teachings of these much revered teacher plants.

I made such a personal choice and traveled to Peru to experience the sacred sites, such as Machu Picchu, and also to spend time in sacred ceremonies with a shaman of amazing depth of heart and integrity of practice. I spent a week touring the sacred sites, preparing myself for a week of ceremonies in the jungle. My attitude was one of a humble student coming to learn what I needed to help me be a better and deeper servant of others.

As a result of my preparation and my deep respect of the shaman and the Spirit Medicine I was blessed with many amazing and humbling experiences during my 10 journeys with Mother Ahyauwasca. These ceremonies took place in a sacred setting in the heart of the Peruvian jungle in the loving and experienced care of an amazing shaman.

Here are a few of my learnings.

Where I put my attention, my life energy, my focus is what I become aware of and what in fact grows. Everything in the universe is happening now in this moment... yes everything. It is all available to each and every one of us now in each magical moment.

The problem is that many of us have been trained to put our attention or focus on matters of survival and the material world. We have just forgotten about the magic and mystery that is around us each and every moment.

What I was taught by Mother Ahyauwasca is all of life is occurring in this exact moment. There is no past or future, simply time all stacked up on top of itself happening in many different realms all in the same moment.

As an individual with choice you do have the power to place your attention on any realm you want. By doing that you can experience the magic each moment has to offer.

She also taught me that practice, persistence and willingness will markedly support spiritual growth. That practice does take time as we all have a lifetime of habits to break. This means that magic happens and mystical event are occurring - it is just that many of us are simply not trained to look for them!

Death is nothing to fear.

Mother Ahyauwasca took me through my own personal death in the body I currently live in. She walked me slowly through each step of my impending death so gently and exquisitely that I was actually able to experience what it will be like to die. It was intense to say the least and yet here I am able to write about it.

She taught me that I as an individual spirit do not die. As a matter of fact if I relax into the experience of my body's death it is actually a joyous celebration and rebirth - an exhale into total freedom. It was a lesson of conscious death, being present at the exact time of letting go of the body. Sure I was scared, frightened to death as we often say. And yet I was able to experience what happens with the final exhale. It was tremendously freeing. You have all heard that you are timeless spiritual beings and that death is nothing to fear, simply a change of status if you will from heavy body to light body. Well, experiencing death first hand in a sacred ceremony breathed **real** life into me!

For me death is now an ally, nothing to be feared, yet a force to be moved by. Knowing death personally has given me a new sense of living my life more fully each and every moment. Like it is my first moment and as if it were my last. Death somehow creates an environment for living a great life.

This experience, though profound and instructive, was not a direct experience. Yes, it most certainly was pure teaching and did align with many of my direct experiences. These ceremonial experiences absolutely support personal spiritual growth by opening doorways to the Great Mystery that we are currently unable to open for ourselves.

Mother Ahyauwasca also taught me not to abuse Her by excessive use, just to trip out in a 'sacred' way. She implored me to take the teachings into my life and put them to practical use, suggesting that once I have embodied what She has taught me I would then be ready for the next level of sacred training. For my money's worth Mother Ahyauwasca is correct.

Be open to the magic and look for it. See it and experience it - it is going on all the time anyway.

Your Children's Safe-keeper

I was driving home from work one day. I was living on BC's Sunshine Coast so the drive was beautiful, rural and ocean side. Rush hour on the Sunshine Coast was about 1 ½ minutes! It was a highway drive undisturbed by street lights or stop signs - a drive full of the riches of ocean views and beautiful forests.

As was my habit back then I was driving in silence, no distractions of the radio, music or tapes. About halfway home I was struck by a profound experience and needed to pull the car over to the side of the highway.

In a moment I was aware that Oliver and Ben, my two boys, were not mine…. That is to say they didn't belong to me. What I became totally aware of was the fact that I was their safe-keeper. Yes, it was my spiritual, sacred responsibility to keep them safe until they could safely take care of themselves.

It may seem odd, it sure seemed odd to me, and yet there was both truth and freedom in it. What I learned was the two young boys were in fact individuals all on their own account, they were equivalent to me in value, no more or no less just because of their size or age. It was my noble job to keep their minds, bodies and spirits safe until such time as they were able to do so for themselves. It fostered in me the desire to honor their already existing independence from me.

Yes, they needed fathering, absolute loving fathering, and yet they also need to 'feel' their own independence, no parental ownership of their young lives. I was sad in the moment as I felt I had lost something… after all they were both under 2 years old and I loved them deeply. It felt a bit as if the Great Mystery had taken them away from me and reclaimed them. I realized though that I was now much freer to raise them as they needed to be raised, as the individual young boys they were, not as clones of me.

Unconditional Love – It really exists

Anjali, my teacher and I had been teaching and giving workshops for about a month here in Vancouver. At the time she was living in Toronto and I had sponsored her coming out west to give enlightenment intensives, provide personal counseling sessions to friends and colleagues, and to offer a week long training program.

We were well through the month of spiritual growth work and both of us deeply satisfied with the events and happenings we had created. We were about half-way through the weeklong training program.. There were 9 participants, Anjali and myself as her staff. I had been actively involved in lots of processes, personal contact with many people - all in a spirit of love and encouragement.

The day was winding down and we had just completed another intense training exercise. I had been involved to make the group even in numbers so each participant would have a partner. The practice was a clearing session where the partner, me, was emptying their mind of stored yet unnecessary thoughts and emotions linked to others in their life. It was and is a powerful technique. As always I was doing the exercise as fully as I could in each moment.

Towards the end of the practice session some magic happened. I was struck in the moment by what I called unconditional love. It was a full blown direct experience of Unconditional Love. In the moment of my opening Anjali called an end to the practice and took all the students away for a debrief of their experience as a practitioner. Meanwhile I was left to my own devices in the midst of my happening with Love.

When the gang returned they found me wrapped in a blanket stuffing Oreo cookies in my face... the ones with the neon colored centers... giggling away with absolute glee!

Anjali took the opportunity to teach the group how to deal with a direct experience and with her skill and experience she supported me in deepening the experience and grounding it firmly in my body. At the end of the day I knew Unconditional Love existed, it is real and palpable. Even though I may not feel it all the time it does not alter the fact that Unconditional Love is... it is simply us who turn away from It.

So it is clear to me that being open to these types of mystical experiences is an important personal choice. These happenings are always occurring; it is simply you and your perspective that keeps you in the dark so to speak. Open to the possibility, to the probability, and you will begin to experience the magic and mystery of life each and every day!

Yet even given these magical, mystical and profound personal experiences, I can and do fall back to sleep in my life. Sometimes the momentum of my history or the intensity of the situation can lull or jar me back into a mindless stupor. It happens all the time to folks just like you too. I have often seen people in moments of direct union with Truth, in blissful aware states only to catch up with them months later, back in the world of tic - toc as Stuart Wilde would say. Struggling yet again with the practice of staying real in the moment - instead being lured by the drama of yesterday or the promise of a better tomorrow.

Heads UP!
Some things to be watching for

Even given all the learning I have experienced, all the practice I have put in and all the study I have completed - life happens. Habitual ways of living run deep and life is all around and going on all the time. The combination of life's inertia and life events themselves can often have the affect of putting us back to sleep - in other words knocking us out of presence and awareness back into reactivity, out of the magical now moment back to the chains of the past or limits of the future. Many of us wake up for moments and then drift unknowingly back to sleep. I am no exception.

One of my alert words or a warning in the form of a feeling is the sense of being settled or "comfortable" in my life. It is like a big comfortable couch in front of a warming fireplace with a great movie on the television. It is that yummy feeling of resting comfortably. Nothing wrong in conscious doses, just not as an ongoing lifestyle though. Well in my life I did slip quietly and unknowingly back into the comfort zone.

Though I have had many amazing experiences over the years and had seemingly developed a good life with lots of Spirit, life had begun nibbling away at my presence and awareness and much like Rip Van Winkle I once again I began to fall asleep at the very switch of my own life.

It was a gradual process, so I didn't really notice the onset of the comfortable zone settling in.   It is a process remarkably similar to hypothermia!

Back to the mind

The more soundly I slumbered – lack of attention and awareness – the worse my life worked. All my accomplishments, all my comforts, all my loves began to crumble. It felt like I had taken a wrong turn down my own life's path.

The more I listened and believed my old thoughts, the more my comfortable life habits kicked in, the worse things got. My wife left me, I lost my employment contracts and part time job, I ultimately lost my money and all the things that I had held onto as security.

As opposed to relying on my direct experiences as a guide, I fell back on past habits and strategies to cope with the intense pressures I felt in my life. You see I was then living a life of a lone wolf and unaccustomed to asking for support. So all the amazing experiences I had became trophies on a shelf instead of principles to live a life by.

I was a cooked goose and asleep at my own switch as once again habits took over.   I returned to my old safety zone, got more education, a Master's Degree. Went back to administration, got a job as an executive director and away I went on auto-pilot.

It was as if all those magical happenings occurred in a dream and I had woken up again to the misery of my poor lot in life. Ugh! So watch out - old habits and lifestyles can and do come roaring back. Make sure you have a circle of friends who will keep an eye on you and offer you real support when you slip off the Path of Truth and Unreasonable Happiness back in to the dreariness of the tic-toc world of north American life as we have come to know it.

Luckily for me another wake up call came my way. This time in the form of a bad car accident.

Another wake up call

I had again fallen prey to the power of my own mind. The inertia of my old life had once again taken over. I found myself back in academia with a Master's Degree in Leadership and Training-honors indeed - and that led me back into the world I had left, the world of administration… a safe place for me to hide.

I took a job as an executive direct of a small non-profit agency in the interior of British Columbia. It was a fine agency and the job was alright. It may have looked like I was back in the swing of things, yet deep in my heart I knew I was running away from the failure of my life. I had found a job hundreds of miles away from friends and more importantly family. I was living in a small cabin in the backwoods away from everyone.

In an odd way it was comfortable. All the while, though, I had a sense it just wasn't the right place for me. I labored with the feeling that I was in the wrong place for all the wrong reasons and to my own peril I chose to ignore it.

One day on the way to a workshop I was leading it happened. Wham! The car I was riding in was rear ended and I suffered severe whiplash. My neck and back were badly damaged and though I did my best to tough it out I was unable to work effectively and at a pace my employer had become accustomed to. I had a hard time sitting or standing for any length of time, my concentration was poor and I had a real challenge functioning day to day.

Ultimately the non-profit agency and I parted ways.

I found myself in my small cabin totally isolated from the world. As I looked at my situation I began to realize why the accident had occurred. I was avoiding the obvious and I knew it. I had actually run away from my life and was trying to start anew, in a way ignoring the fact I had a previous life that included an ex-wife and kids who were a 10 hour drive away.

I knew deep in my heart I needed to be back in Vancouver closer to my children, friends and family. Yet I was unable to make that choice consciously, continued to live from my history and old habits despite all my spiritual experiences.

My own mind is an impressive foe.

The car accident gave me the bang on the head I needed in order to come to my senses, to wake up again and see what I really needed to do in my life. Yes it was a damaging wake up call, yet it was exactly what I needed in order to get back to living more Truth in my life. It actually knocked me out of my mind and back into my heart.

I spent two and a half months alone in my cabin pondering my future and what I needed to do from my heart. What was it I was aching to do? It was a painful yet amazing time for me as I searched my soul for my next step.

I was looking for work of course all the while and continually came up empty handed – unusual for me as I had always been able to find work when I wanted to. One day in the late afternoon it came to me clear as a bell. Move back to Vancouver, you will find work easily and be closer to home! I was being called home to family and friends, back to the life I had run from in shame.

The very next morning I packed what few belongings I had and left for Vancouver. I never looked back. Two days after arriving in Vancouver I had found a place to live and I obtained a good job in the social services field. My friends and family were only an hour and a bit away. I was home and happy to be there.

Car accident or wakeup call…hmmm?

Back to service

So I took this 'accident' as a wake up call and threw myself back into my spiritual practice of serving others in real life… doing my best to support people in creating an abundant, full passionate life for themselves. I followed my heart's deepest calling of working with people individually. It is what I loved to do and what I wanted to do more than anything… so I just did it!

I took all that I knew, all that I was trained to do, mixed it in with my heart's driving passion and poured myself into social work in the downtown east side of Vancouver. I was glad to be back working directly with people and it showed… I was happy! It also showed in my work. People I worked with were actually being helped.

I was back on my path of loving service following as best I could my deepest purpose as I knew it.

I truly enjoyed what I was still doing for a living, yet it lacked something for me. Something in me still wasn't fully expressed through my chosen work. I was feeling the need for something deeper and more spiritual. Something that would have my soul more deeply satisfied.

What was going on here was my deepest purpose was shifting a bit. Yes, I was serving others as best I could, and I was doing some good in the world. There was a nagging feeling in my heart, though, that I had more to give to people in a more direct way.

So I tracked my friend and teacher, Anjali down and asked her what was up in her world. I was glad to find out that she was still leading Enlightenment Intensives and that our mutual friend Satyen was running a small company that was offering personal growth workshops in western Canada including Vancouver.

So I continued to follow my heart and began volunteering for WarriorSage. I staffed several workshops with them and found myself even happier in my life. I had a good job in social services that allowed me to serve people in a helpful way and earn a living to pay my bills. I also was very fortunate to have a viable spiritual outlet of service through volunteering. Happy and satisfied I was. My life was full and I was feeling very much alive at the edge of my skills and abilities. My life of services was working! So I did more of it!

Then one day I arrived at a significant fork in my road. This is a place many of us arrive at regularly though at varying degrees of consciousness or awareness. Satyen, the owner of WarriorSage called and offered me full time work with WarriorSage, an upstart workshop company.

Hmmm... a secure well paying union job with benefits and an RRSP contribution on the one hand and an offer from an upstart spiritual growth personal development company...
Hmmm... security versus uncertainty...
Hmmm... heart versus mind...
Hmmm... planned and safe versus passion and purpose...

Sometimes the heart wins, caution is thrown to the wind and deep purpose shows up. I took the job offer.

Living life on a path of service with a great wife, good friends and wonderful opportunities to serve others, to grow personally as well as earning a good income, I have never felt so alive, so on purpose and so uncertain about the future. Sometime a man needs to follow his heart not his 'common' sense. This was absolutely my case and I have never looked back.

And yes, for you realists out there, it has been one heck of a roller coaster ride. All manner of challenges and opportunities. Wonderful travel to far-away exotic places and the absolute joy of working intimately with people.

Wouldn't change it!

They are all doing it for my sake. A modern day mantra
In our culture I have found it is common and usual for people to blame others for their lot in life. We do it well here in North America. The Blame Game can sound like this: It is the fault of the economy or the prime minister or president's fault.   It is my wife's fault for not being _____. Fill in the blank. It is my child's fault for not doing _____. Fill in the blank. It is God's fault for not providing _____. Fill in the blank. I have discovered this habitual practice handcuffs personal spiritual growth. There is no way out if you take this popular perspective.

Ultimately it leads to failure and loss time after time. You see, when you blame someone else for your failure or lack you have given your personal power over to them. You will forever be in their control… they will make you happy or they will make you sad, or they will make you _____. Just fill in the blank.

I have learned through the years that there is only one way out of this downward spiraling codependent mess. Take personal responsibility for where you are at.

This particular message has been spoken by many spiritual and personal growth teachers; it is not new. What I have added is this seemingly little twist. Whenever I have a personal reaction to someone else's behavior, instead of acting on my reactivity I internally chant the following mantra;

"They are doing it for my sake."

I can hear the questions already. It goes against all our conditioning. And yet it is working well for me. "They are doing it for my sake"… doesn't let the others off the hook, what it does is it lets Me off the hook. If I am reactive and someone pushes my buttons I should celebrate them and thank them for supporting me in looking closely at my reactivity. Underneath my reactivity is a closely held belief about myself. When brought out into the light of day by someone other than me I can then actually work with it and shed some light on it. Ultimately I become free of that belief that had previously kept me locked up in a jail of reactivity.

In handling reactivity in this way you can actually become master over your own neurotic beliefs and attitudes, attitudes that keep you totally separate from others and from love.

Attached to this mantra is a sequel, "What is it about me?" So you simply turn the finger you are pointing at the other right back at you. You see we are really here for each other's awakening and reactivity to me confirms this. We are all conspiring to wake each other up and will do all manner of things to do just that.

This practice of "They are doing it for my sake." will lead you right into your own mind and how you co-create those very situations that upset you and cause you to stay attached unconsciously to others. For me it is one of the most powerful ways to free yourself from the bars of my own mind.

Time to be real about all this.
A sober look at things mystical
At some point as individuals we need to rest and to review what we have done, what we have learned, how we have lived and what we have

accomplished. In the spiritual realm it is a close personal review of how we have directed our lives based on the experiences we have had... especially those experiences deemed mystical.

It is much like the four seasons, spring, summer, fall and winter. We plant and nurture in the spring, we fertilize and water in the summer. In the fall we harvest with gratitude the crops that have resulted from our efforts – we celebrate. In the winter we rest and get ready for the next spring.

It is the phase where experiences are reviewed. It is a time when we evolve the heart. Worldly and mystical experience purified by the heart turn from data to a heartfelt natural wisdom. This time of the sage is an important stage and once well underway gives the warrior energy much more balance, much more authentic power.

In First Nations Culture it is the phase of the elder. In my culture, white Anglo-Saxon, it is the age of the grandfather.

It is a time of reflection and deeper understanding – the time of the sage.

Mystical Experiences in Review

So let's take a closer look at these experiences from the first opening on June 20, 1988 until those of this past year. Let's play a bit and see what we can create out of all these experiences, states, realizations and profound openings to Truth. Let us see how they play out - how the meditative states link with spirit medicine states connect with life states and lead to living a life based on spirit.

I will weave in some of the thinking of several great philosophers and mystics who have given us some amazing teachings. William James, Ghandi, Robert Greenleaf to name a few.

The overall theme is that individual experiences of Truth, illumination, enlightenment, satori or whatever you wish to call them are a personal matter - the reality of them indisputable. The certainty of these experiences can and should be relied upon more than the words of others written into some sort of philosophy.

As Simon Buxton says, "Let's explore this zone of the soul!"

Mystical Experience 1
It is All connected, We are all One

Well it was as if everything was connected, connected to me. All smells, all sounds, all sights, all things sensory seemed to be totally happening in me or me in them. There was simply no separation between me and light, me and sound, me and fragrance, me and other than me. I couldn't tell if I was hearing the sound in my head or where the noise originated. It was as if the image I saw was both in me and outside of me at the same time. Everything I had held as other than me was now totally in me, of me, as me. Isolation, separation, feeling alone or closed was absolutely not the case.

I understood in that timeless moment all the teachings of the Great Ones; Jesus, Gandhi, Martin Luther King,

Mother Teresa, Lao Tzu, and Jehovah.

I knew everything. I was living in the Tao.

I was all things, all time. I was absolutely everything and nothing all in the same moment.

Mystical Experience 2
Life is always exactly what each of us needs

I stood there in apparent silence, everything motionless, and no one moving even a finger. Much like a movie video put on pause – the frame was frozen – except for me.

I stood there in breathless silence. My eyes fell on my father who was working for the same company, Burns Fry Ltd., on the same floor, the 50th floor of First Canadian Place, and in the same department Fixed Income. As I gazed at him my entire life played before me. I could see all the twists and turns, all the subconscious choices, all the events that took place to get me there. All this occurred to have me at this exact place at this exact time so I could learn what I needed to. So I could let go of the past and move on in my life. My path to this exact moment was absolutely clear. There were no mistakes, no wrong turns, and no flukes. My entire life to this point was perfect!

Mystical Experience 3
The entire universe exists in me!

It made absolutely no sense, but as I reopened to the truth it just kept pouring into me. I am the space between all things. I am that in which all of life happens. I am without boundaries. I am pure existence the consciousness that everything happens in.

I was struck with an extreme headache as my mind and the direct experience clashed. How I had thought of myself what I believed about me was totally smashed by what I had just 'learned'. So profound was the truth and so in opposition to my beliefs it was like my entire life's foundation was shattered by this one mystical experience.

No matter how much my history and my mind fought against it, the truth of what I was unrelentingly continued to show up in my contemplation. The absolute certainty I had was mind blowing... I was in fact nothing but space, that empty consciousness in which all existence occurred!

There was no question about it. I was the space between all things.

In the same instant it was as if I was timeless. I was the tick between the seconds, that absolute place of no time at all. I felt I had always existed and always would.

Mystical Experience 4
I am God.

> *Later on the final day of the Intensive during the last*
> *walking contemplation I was overcome by another*
> *splash in the truth. I felt the utter divinity of me, the*
> *absolute sacredness of who I was. The words that*
> *came out of my mouth were I am a child of God.*

> *No, no I am God.*

> *I could barely catch my breath; I was stunned by the*
> *experience. I had always thought that God had an*
> *office, or was something to bow down to, an absolute*
> *authority to which I could pray. But God and I were*
> *of the same essence!*

So what you might say is all these mystical experiences are fine but
what good are they?

Excellent question!

They can be kept as trophies like animal heads hung on a wall or sports
trophies keep in a trophy case. If that is how you handle your experiences
it means precious little to the world. Many times these experience are
philosophized, categorized, and turned into some sort of doctrine or have
some sort of institution created around them.

However, I want to demonstrate that our individual mystical experiences can lead to freedom and a capacity to live a passionate, compassionate and powerful life. Each one of us can become our own individual that takes the leadership reins when it works for the overall good of the family, community and world we live in.

I am making the point here that if each one of us is ready, willing, and able we could turn the world upside down and re-write the literature on community leadership!

Imagine these four simple experiences being lived fully in my life, so you can see how you could live more fully your own experiences in your own life. Here are the four examples of my experiences:

1) It is All connected, we are all One.
2) Life is always exactly what each of us needs.
3) The entire universe exists in me!
4) I am God.

Now here are some areas of everyday life that could be fully affected if these four simple direct or mystical experiences were lived fully.

In the arena of interpersonal communications just imagine if I treated others as if they were me… we are all one and treated them like the God they actually are. Then add a touch of **life is always exactly what each of us needs.**

There would be no problems to fix, no one is broken and every one is experiencing exactly what they need to grow and evolve as a spiritual individual having a human experience. We would automatically listen and speak with love as we are a God communicating with another God. We would practice the art of true understanding and stop trying to get others to simply agree with us.

We would make contact with each other in a way that demonstrated our oneness. There would be a field of love generated between those that were in contact and communication with each other if we all practiced these four experiences.

The reality factor in our lives would go through the roof. Many of us really want more authenticity in our lives, we want each other to be real. Well, in living these truths more fully there would be more Truth spoken, heard and lived. The simple fact that we would speak our individual truth unedited and with love would transform all relationships overnight.

What is more… imagine if we spoke to each other as if we were all God.

These four simple Truths, if lived fully, would transform the lifestyle we all live here in North America. We are, most of us, locked into living the dull side of the North American Dream, the dream we have all been manipulated into believing in. Get a good job, make money, get married and have children, pay your taxes and retire in happiness. Look at what has happened: debt, collapsing economies, global recession, housing and stock prices in the trash can and job loss.

Many of us are frightened to death by the goings-on around us, frozen in the grip of fear that there are not enough jobs, money or opportunities. Holding on for dear life all the while crushing the joy, happiness, creativity and spirit out of ourselves.

If you know:
1) **It is All connected, we are all One.**
2) **Life is always exactly what each of us needs.**
3) **The entire universe exists in me!**
4) **I am God.**

Would you be so fearful? No - you would all be free to live your lives as you choose, in spite of what we see going on around us. This may not necessarily change the economics of the day. It could change how we respond as conscious spiritual beings living a human existence. As a conscious being we would all have the capacity and ability to breathe and open through the events of the day and make choices from our natural free loving existence and not from abject fear and panic.

A different choice? Of course...

Imagine if we all dropped the notion that there is an authority outside of us that has supreme knowledge wisdom and power over us. It would change the way we relate to our employers, our education system, our legal system and even our president or prime minister.

If these four simple Truths of mine were lived fully how would a president govern his people? How would an employer treat her employees? More to the point how would each of us allow ourselves to be treated by the folks we tend to put in high places. What if Obama is just like you? What if he is simply doing a different job than any one of us?

What would happen if we treated these so called superstars just like our next door neighbor and they returned the favor? Are we letting ourselves off the hook by putting these "demi-gods" up on a pedestal? Are we abrogating our own personal responsibility and inner passion and enabling others to fulfill them for us? Do we then blame them when they let us down? Be wary of this one! The slippery slope of adoration or repulsion.

What is more painful is why we do not put ourselves up on the same pedestal… imagine if we all raised ourselves up in this way? Or imagine if we all went out and played the sport we were watching on television with the children in our neighborhood? Imagine if we took our politics genuinely and instead of complaining about our political leaders we took an active role in the redevelopment of our neighborhoods, communities, towns, cities and countries at large?

The Now moment … where we all really live anyway

Imagine living without a past to hold you back or a future to keep you worried. Imagine simply living in each moment as if it were fresh and new. Just take a close look at each of your days and notice how much time you spend bringing up the past and using it to color your experience in the moment, using the past to justify how you feel about someone and something that they always or never do.

Notice how much time you spend thinking or worrying about the future. Does this future thinking take you totally out of each precious now moment? "Oh I know he will do this." You bank on it and in a way force to happen exactly what you are dreading.

If you really take a close look at this past future thinking you will become clear on why magic and abundance are lacking in your life. You see these two realities, magic and abundance, are always happening. However they only occur in the exquisiteness of the Now moment. If we are busy thinking or pondering the past, or thinking and worrying about the future we are missing the point.   The point is Now is where all exists.   Imagine living as if there was no past or is no future, simply living in each beautiful now moment.

Wow!

> *"No mind is much employed upon the present*
> *moment; Recollection and anticipation fill up almost*
> *all of our moments."*
> *~Samuel Johnson*

– Section Three –
Putting it All Together
Life and Spirituality

How could it all look?

How could families, communities and businesses work in an even more loving and inclusive way? Could neighborhoods function with even more reality, compassion, freedom and love? What could happen if we all began living from our deepest awakenings, insights and realizations?

What could leadership look like?
Some stock definitions of leadership...

> *Leadership has been defined organizationally and narrowly as "the ability of an individual to influence, motivate, and enable others to contribute toward the effectiveness and success of the organizations of which they are members." Organizationally, leadership directly impacts the effectiveness of costs, revenue generation, service, satisfaction, earnings, market value, share price, social capital, motivation, engagement, and sustainability. Leadership is the ability of an individual to set rules for others and lead from the front. It is an attitude that influences the environment around us.*
> *~From Wikipedia, the free encyclopedia*

Here is another take on a definition of leadership. It comes from the book Fifth Discipline – Field Book by Peter Senge.

> *"In the realm of leadership, many people are conditioned to see our 'organizations' as things rather than as patterns of interaction. We look for solutions that will 'fix problems' as if they are external and can be fixed without 'fixing' that which is within us that led to their creation.*
> *~Peter Senge*

Here is a definition of leadership that is short and to the point!

> *"The first responsibility of a leader is to define reality. The last is to say thank you. In between, the leader is a servant."*
> *~ Max DePree*

A different definition...

> *Leadership is a dynamic, collective energy that ought not to be confined to a single position or individual. True leadership flows through individuals in families, communities or organizations no matter what their position. Leadership is not a job or title. It is a creative series of personal interactions in service to the overall good*
> *~Stephen Garrett*

I remember as a young child playing with a toy that reminds me of practical spiritual leadership. It was a tool bench kind of affair with a bunch of posts of different shapes placed in openings of the same shape. As I banged one post down another post popped up. As I banged that one down a different post would pop up. It was never-ending, always a post popping up as one was being banged down.

In a healthy family, community or organization, leadership could look much the same – different individuals popping up to share in the spontaneous flow of leadership.

Leadership in Companies

This form of leadership flow may at first seem chaotic, and yet it is going on all the time anyway! Just look at the organization you work in! Look beyond the so-called head of things and see what is going on behind her. There is suppressed or unrecognized, unacknowledged leadership in all its myriad forms. We often put negative labels on these leaders because of two things - the way they bring their leadership to the group and more importantly what they bring. The reason we often label others is they bring forward issues leaders would rather not deal with.

Here are the labels we oftentimes put on unacknowledged leadership:

The Ball Buster – The Whistle Blower - Office Gossip
Water Cooler Meeting Dude – The Yes Man
The Complainer – I Told You So – The Partier
The Green Nag – The Eternal Optimist – Mister I Don't
Give a Shit – The Policy Cop – Corporate Miser
The Pessimist

Each of these individuals could play a significant role in the leadership of a family, community, or organization if only we would recognize their unique approach to their style of leadership. Instead we label them, judge them, and in a way put them in 'their' place. This all goes on and is easily seen for those who are willing to look. This negative approach to dynamic and organic leadership is the bane of modern organizations, communities and families.

Let me show you a different approach to these so called trouble-makers. For the sake of simplicity I will focus on the organizational role each play and you can overlay the explanation to community and family easily – I'll give you an example or two of how to do this.

I will describe how the label is most often viewed in an organization and then I will show you the 'other' side of the coin. You see I believe in looking for the **positive intent** of people that underlies, most often unconsciously, their behavior. I have found that when I do look for this positive intent two things happen... I find it... and I can see past the label to what the person is really trying to offer the organization.

So here we go, let us look at the Complainer and the Pessimist in some detail then I will table the remaining leadership negative labels with their positive intent so you can all get the hang of this new way of looking for genuine leadership by turning it inside out.

The Complainer, when looked at through the lenses of positive intent, really does care about the organization, family or neighborhood otherwise they would not invest their time in complaining... complaining takes effort, time, and willingness. The complainer is also gutsy because of the typical reaction to complaints and the complainer. Most often complaints are reluctantly received and the complainer is oftentimes treated in a bit of a dismissive way.

Imagine if the complaint and the complainer were welcomed and received with open arms… this is the power of positive intent. Ultimately the complainer would get that their unique style of leadership was valued and the complaining energy would be transformed into a management style that would be happily received, effective, and transformative. You see the complaint is always about improvement. It just has a bit of negative energy associated with it. Once the positive intent is spotted and spoken out loud by the receiver the complainer seems to magically change into a *quality control leader!*

The Pessimist when looked at through the eyes of positive intent also mysteriously transforms into a *solution oriented planner.* The pessimist sees all possibilities and is concerned that the general leadership team is missing some of the possibilities that are not so positive… those outcomes that would be disastrous if the were not looked at and included in managements decision-making process.

The pessimist simply wants leadership to include and be prepared for all possibilities even though they may never occur. The pessimist simply does not want to get blind-sided. When this wider view is laced with negative emotion the pessimist is usually energetically dismissed along with the possibilities they have the capacity to see. When we are able to spot and acknowledge the positive intent of the pessimist we can then easily add their wider view of possibilities to the mix and be a much better prepared organization. When the pessimist is acknowledged in this way for their more expansive vision they somehow magically transform into a wonderful *solution oriented planner!*

Stereo Typical Label	Positive Intent Title
The Ball Buster	Keeping It Real Manager
The Whistle Blower	Manager of Integrity
Office Gossip	Communication Officer
Water Cooler Meetings Dude	Informal Staff Debrief Chief
The Yes Man	Vice President of Making it Happen
I Told You So	Company Historian
The Office Drunk	Manager of Timely Celebrations
The Green Nag	Officer of Paying Attention
The Eternal Optimist	Manager of Positive Intent
The Policy Cop	Manager of Healthy Boundaries
The Corporate Miser	Vice President of Abundance

So the new art form of looking for positive intent will transform the energy surrounded in the old titles and labels of trouble makers into true, organic, in-the-moment leadership. The simple adjustment from negative to positive will almost immediate turn all decisions into amazing results.

Leadership is Upside Down and Inside Out
A True Leader is Responsible for the Abundance of their Staff

When I take a close look at leadership whether in a family, community, or company, I see it all as upside down. In most structures the boss is on top. She is on top in position, in responsibility, authority and also in remuneration. The structure is designed to ensure that the top dog reaps the rewards.

It has been this way for millennia and it has been a successful structure for those on top. It has worked well in many ways. However it has kept a lid on real leadership.

Get the idea of a pyramid in it's current position – a broad flat base rising to a peak... this is the structure of current leadership models in most cases. The entire structure is designed to support the peak.

In my world the pyramid ought to be turned upside down and the peak should support the rest of the structure. In more corporate words the CEO should be beneath all his employees ensuring that each one of them has everything they need to be successful and abundant in all they do each and every day.

The CEO should be totally responsible for the well being of all her charges, making sure that everyone above her is growing and evolving as a fully responsible leader the their company, organization or family. The full weight of the organization should fall squarely on the shoulders of the one most responsible and it should be shouldered with a humble and joyful pride.

This change in leadership perspective would result in most companies doing much better financially, they would have happier clients and a more successful financial result for all involved!

Leadership in Community

Leadership in its less evolved forms create all manner of problems as seen in today's financial melt down and the greed demonstrated by those 'leaders' at the top of some corporate organizations. It also shows up in other areas such as religions and social service agencies. Social Services you ask? Yes, even here we can see leadership run amuck even though it may appear on the surface heartfelt.

You see the corporate gang seem to have less heart and more drive for profit. The social services group has lots of heart for sure and usually lack the necessary business drive. In both cases **long term vision for the good of all people** needs to be taken into account.

It is easy to pick apart the more common corporate leadership style that has been mired down in money and greed. It has been well documented throughout this past economic melt down so we need not review it here. However, let's take a look at social services through a different set of lenses and see what is really underlying this style of leadership and how we could change it for the better of all.

In my experience of some thirteen years it appears to me that social services are in fact co-dependent and self perpetuating. I have spent time in the world of social services on many different levels, from a home support worker to an executive director and as a board member as well. My observations are based on what I saw going on from these multiple perspectives.

Initially I was moved to the world of social service because of my great compassion for people. Many of the individuals I had the pleasure of working with in this field were motivated initially by the same deep sense of compassion. This sense of compassion is the root of community service.

In the early days community services would pop up to support a specific need in a community. Once their service had been delivered and the social wrong righted they would simple dissolve the movement with a fine celebration. Over time, though, what happened was the movement of compassion for others turned into a self-fulfilling permanent agency or social services society such as we have today. These agencies are now obliged in a way to maintain themselves by seeking causes (funding) to ensure they keep their doors open and employees paid.

This is all noble and yet from my vantage point has me asking – "Why do we still need all these social service agencies? Haven't they had enough time to get the job done?"

Here are some of my thoughts:
Social services have created by their very ongoing existence a co-dependent attitude of entitlement amongst the very people they are attempting to support.

Social service agencies have professionalized the skills and abilities that used to be common in families and communities. In a way they have robbed communities of the very skills they need to support themselves, then turn around and 'rent' these same skills back to the people they took them from. (By rent I mean these agencies rely on public funding, tax payers dollars, for their livelihood.)

The relationship between the agency and its clients is fraught with co-dependence. Each party needs the other in order to exist. So the agency in some kind of weird unconscious way keeps their clients stuck in the rut of poverty and neediness.

Can you grasp what I am talking about here?

Conscious, awakened leadership in the social service setting would look very different if they took to heart some basic and fundamental Truths. I would venture to say that we would not have a need for this long term expensive solution to many social problems if we approached these social opportunities from a different viewpoint.

What could the world of social services look like if they took the approach that they would be out of business within five years as a leadership mandate? Out of business because they had done such an amazing job 'teaching' people how as opposed to the current view of long term support.

What would happen if agency staff treated their clients as spiritual adults not needy 'children' and simply returned the professionalized skills to community and family members.

Here is an example of what I am encouraging here.

I spent several years in the hospice field of social services and I loved the work... I deeply honor and value those others who served with me. Yet wouldn't it be better if we trained family members, neighbors and community members to offer the same service naturally just as a part of real community living. What happens now in many communities is when death strikes a family the first reaction is to call in the professionals that have the skill to help.

It is good to ask for help and support – it would be even better if that same support flowed naturally from friends and neighbors who have all the hospice skills they need lying dormant in their bodies. I have seen community and neighborly support around death happen spontaneously and beautifully in the rare community and it was a joy to witness.

Meals cooked, children cared for, dear ones consoled, and arrangements handled - understanding, compassion and love flowing generously from family members and neighbors who 'know' how to care for each other during times of transition like death.

If I were Prime Minister I would ensure that all social services agencies were happily out of business in 10 years time!

Leadership in Family - Some Maxims of Spiritual Life

Here in point form are some interesting practices we can all put into play in our daily lives. I know that when you do, magic will begin to show up everywhere!

1. Put yourself second, put the other first.

2. Remember that the person you are having an upset with is not their behavior or reaction. Make loving contact with the divine individual first, then discuss the situation. Love them, not the behavior.

3. Turn towards the upset, stay in the fire with each other. Do not turn away.

4. Take your time and never give up.

5. Flood others with love and joy.

6. Don't sweat the small stuff, remember the bigger picture of love and freedom.

7. Treat each other as divine beings.

8. Live each day and each moment as if it will be your last.

9. How do you want to be remembered and for what? Let this question lead your daily activities.

Gratitude and Service will arise naturally as we begin to live fully what we have learned through these mystical experiences. It is the daily practice of our own spiritual awakenings that propel us into the magical life of genuine gratitude and selfless services. It is this ultimate combination that will set you all free from the life of self... self-centered... self-indulgent... self-righteous. Where you place your attention is what grows, remember that one? Simply place your loving attention on others and watch them grow.

It's good to base a life on service and gratitude. The more I do so in my life the more amazing my life becomes.

Try it!

I know you will love it!

Unusual Looks at some 'Accepted' Realities

Leadership in Government – Democracy?

Many of us think that we are living in a democratic society. We get to elect our leaders, municipally, provincially and federally. Have a good look though – look a little deeper than the surface and you may see what I have seen.

Are we truly living in a democratic society? Do we really get to choose our Prime Minister or are we accepting what the parties offer us? Perhaps it is really feudalism cloaked in the garb of democracy. Which system are we really living in? Here are a couple of definitions that may help in the discussion.

Democracy

Even though there is no universally accepted definition of 'democracy' there are two principles that any definition of democracy includes. The first principle is that all members of the society (citizens) have equal access to power and the second that all members (citizens) enjoy universally recognized freedoms and liberties.

Feudalism

Feudalism, by its very nature, gave rise to a hierarchy of rank, to a predominantly static social structure in which every man knew his place, according to whom it was that he owed service and from whom it was that he received his land. In order to preserve existing relationships in perpetuity, rights of succession to land were strictly controlled by various laws, or customs, of entail.

Every man was the vassal, or servant, of his lord. The man swore fealty to his lord, and in return the lord promised to protect him and to see that he received justice. Feudalism was the expression of a society in which every man was bound to every other by mutual ties of loyalty and service. Feudal society was characterized by military landholders and working peasants. The nobility included bishops, for the church was one of the greatest of medieval landowners. Near the bottom of the social pyramid were the agricultural laborers, and beneath them, the serfs.

So which one is it? Democracy or Feudalism?

Answer… Feudalism is correct!

Now for my money's worth I am heading for the following form of government - one not seen in North America.

Anarchy

A social state in which there is no governing person or group of persons, but each individual has absolute liberty (without the implication of disorder).

This aligns nicely with my personal belief in taking personal responsibility for one's own life. It is the only way to truly practice empowerment. I am also seriously tired of follower-ship, besides the boat is sinking! I am much more excited about creating a world that is leader-full.

What's going on with my tax money?

"Why is it that the bulk of my annual taxes go to the most distant level of government," I asked? In my country, Canada, our federal government in Ottawa receives the bulk of my tax money. Yet it is damn impossible for me to talk to my member of parliament never mind chatting with the prime minister.

The next big chunk of my tax payments goes to the provincial government and it is equally difficult to get in touch with my member of the legislative assembly never mind the premier.

Yet the mayor of Langley, the municipality I live in, is infinitely easy to find. In a way we are neighbors and if need be I could easily track the mayor down. Yet Langley gets a very small portion of my tax dollars.

Wouldn't it make sense to have the largest part of my taxes go to the place nearest me so I can better see how the political folks handle my money?

You are not buying anything – you are investing in the seller's life style
Get the idea whenever you purchase a good or a service that you are in fact enabling the seller to live the life they are living.

Then ask the question – Can I support that life style? What principles do they live by?

Vote with your money – because you are anyway.

Be mindful when you spend. You ought to know who you are supporting.

Entitlement versus Personal Action

Pervasive in our culture these days is the unconscious energy of entitlement. I have seen it in all walks of life. We most often point a finger at those in receipt of government social support and in many cases there is truth there. I have sensed this underlying belief that I deserve welfare or I deserve my unemployment assistance, my boss owes me a pay check, as if it is an individual right.

There is also a belief amongst the mid to high income earners that I deserve what I have, I am entitled to big income because I have gone to university, I have put in my time, I come from the right family. There is a strand of entitlement here too!

This attitude, somebody somewhere owes me something, is rampant in our culture here in North America. Sometimes it is visible, most often it is operating below the level of conscious awareness. This very attitude acknowledged or not is totally depriving many of us of our own individual personal power to create that which we need in our lives.

Nobody owes any of us anything!

And here is the ultimate cop-out.

There is No God Almighty!

The ultimate abrogation of personal responsibility (cop-out) is that there exists a God who sits in judgment of how we have lived our lives. This God has some sort of final say. You go to heaven and you go to hell. Though it may not be spoken this bluntly there is a sense in most religions of this type of superior father who will ultimately save our sorry souls.

We then act out this basic core belief through our educational systems, our financial systems, our system of government and especially our religious systems. We are often pointing a finger at or blaming some higher authority for our lot in life. You can notice these phenomena all around you. Simply listen for phrases like these:

"It is the boss' fault I lost my job."

"The president should fix the economy, and our education system."

"You make me angry!"

"I can't be happy on my own."

"I can't help it."

You will notice all these claims are pointing the finger at someone outside of yourself – all based on the foundational cellular belief that there is a God who will save you!

This may seem like a huge stretch to link the belief in a God with the blame game and yet it is so clearly self-evident.

The only way to personal power, freedom and Love is to take total personal responsibility for all of your life! Yes - everything in your life good, bad and ugly! Below is an article I recently wrote for an E-zine called Radiant Lights... it follows the same theme.

Spirituality Is Anarchy
Imagine That

One of the most subtle ways we all defer our personal power to another or to others is a belief in an almighty God. This particular belief is so subtle and powerful that it lies under all our social, corporate, governmental and familial structures. Simply have a look see.

There is always the head honcho of almost any organized unit you wish to study… usually father in a family, mayor of a community, president of a company, executive director of a social services agency and a prime minister or president of a country… a God of the universe.

In this way we all undermine our own personal power and become a type of quiet follower. We put our X in a ballot box, accept a pay cheque, pay taxes, or put money in the church collection box. In each of these ways we are handing over our personal power to an authority we have subtly or not so subtly put above ourselves. We believe that someone above will ultimately take good care of us… our government pension, God at the gates of heaven, Dad when we need a few extra bucks.

Just look at it with fresh eyes and you will see!

Here are two 'definitions' if you will, read them both:

Spiritual; *When a person to refer to himself as more spiritual than religious it implies relative deprecation of rules, rituals, and traditions while preferring an intimate relationship with 'God'. Their basis for this belief is that Jesus Christ came to free man from those rules, rituals, and traditions, giving them the ability to walk in the spirit thus maintaining a spiritual lifestyle through that one-to-one relationship with God.*

Anarchy; *A social state in which there is no governing person or group of persons, but each individual has absolute liberty (without the implication of disorder).*

I have always thought of myself as spiritual and always made a clear defining break between religious and spiritual. I believe this distinction is correct, yet in my own life I am sometimes still waiting for a 'higher power' to save my sorry butt!

What happens if there is no God, no higher power, no real boss?
What happens if we are all of equivalent power and that we are all God if you will?
What happens if we each have our own ultimate say?

Anarchy is the answer, simple, practical, spiritual anarchy. It may sound chaotic, crazy and way out there yet how else could each of us reclaim our profound personal power to create our own individual universes that dance in some sort of holographic, spontaneous, harmony with all others without the current cadre of structures, rules and doctrines.

These very structures we have built by our own participation are the very bars that hold us all captured in personal prisons of dutiful follower-ship. Where are you in prison, in a role that restricts you or holds you small? Where do you hide behind God Almighty quietly hoping that heaven will be better than life? Where do you play the **If Only Game**? *Where do you play the* **Blame Game**?

Welcome to 2012:

Spiritual Anarchy
Community Life for the Brave of Heart
and
Fearless in Action.

Community is becoming the next great leader.

Closing Notes

And in the end the love you take is equal to the love you make.
  ~The Beatles

At the end of the day whether or not we have other lifetimes, it is how we
have loved, how we have cared and how we have acted
that forms our legacy.

It is not so much the things we have built
because ultimately they all crumble,
more it is
how we treated others as we built.

It is not so much the money we amassed
it is
how generous we were with our abundance.

It is not so much whether we loved
it is
was our love contagious.

It is not so much how free we lived
it is
did our living help others live their lives with more freedom.

We are all already free, we are all already love,
and we are already the great mystery.

So tag,
YOU are it...

The Artist of Love and Freedom.

PASS IT ON!

– About WarriorSage –

The Path of The WarriorSage is for those who want their personal and spiritual growth fast, and without the 'fluff' of New Age thinking. It is for you if you are willing to do what it takes to really make a huge difference in your life, and eventually in the lives of those you love, and beyond that even to serving the world open with your Awakened WarriorSage heart, skills, and insights.

The Warrior within You is that part of you that faces, feels, and moves through your fears with Courage, Openness, Honesty, Humility, and heart, and does whatever it takes, despite obstacles, to realize your goals.

The Sage within You is that part of you that, with one foot in the World and one foot in the Mystery, is able to play, laugh, and love through life.

The WarriorSage within You is that part of you that lives with the Intention, Courage, Action and Endurance of the Warrior combined fluidly with the Humour, Transcendence, Wisdom and Love of the Sage.

www.warriorsage.com
(800) 815-1545

– Spreading the Word –

OK Now What Do I Do?

Personally I don't believe in wonder books or lifesaving workshops - they in and of themselves don't work. I have found this to be true in my own life. I have read hundreds of books and taken scores of workshops. But what really worked for me was when I began to take the information and apply it in my life.

So you have read my book and learned a few things about how you can lead a more passionate life full of personal freedom and love. That's great, and don't leave your insights, understandings and learnings in the book by your bedside. Begin by taking action in your life now…

Here is what you can do next.

The pages that follow include an amazing gift for you to take full advantage of. There is an amazing gift certificate and a remarkable offer.

The Illumination Intensive Five Day program with a tuition value of $1,997.00 is yours tuition FREE. All you are responsible for is the cost of your meals and accommodation plus a small administration fee. This world class event has seen hundreds of people…

This gift is worth $3,394.00!

Don't delay as this workshop will help you change your life for the better. **Call our office today and register for The Illumination Intensive!**

WarriorSage Inc.
1 (800) 815-1545

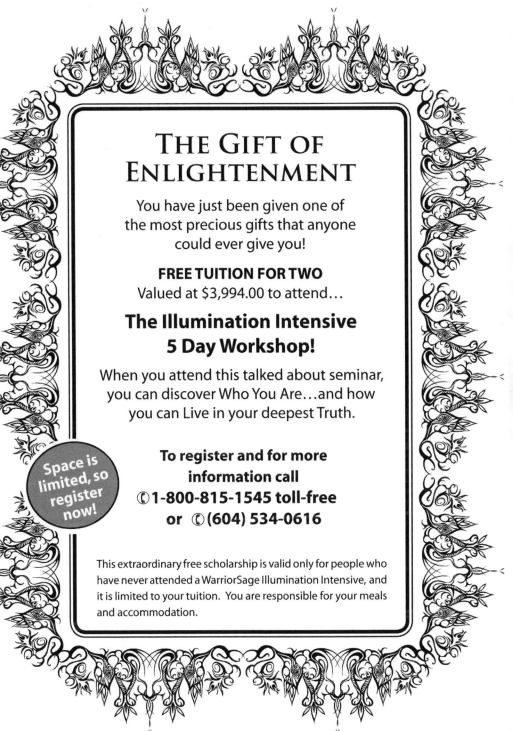

THE GIFT OF ENLIGHTENMENT

You have just been given one of the most precious gifts that anyone could ever give you!

FREE TUITION FOR TWO
Valued at $3,994.00 to attend…

The Illumination Intensive 5 Day Workshop!

When you attend this talked about seminar, you can discover Who You Are…and how you can Live in your deepest Truth.

To register and for more information call
℃ 1-800-815-1545 toll-free
or ℃ (604) 534-0616

Space is limited, so register now!

This extraordinary free scholarship is valid only for people who have never attended a WarriorSage Illumination Intensive, and it is limited to your tuition. You are responsible for your meals and accommodation.